SOPHOMORE SLUMP

SOPHOMORE SLUMPS

Disastrous Second Movies, Albums, Singles, Books, and Other Stuff

by Christopher Golden

A CITADEL PRESS BOOK
Published by Carol Publishing Group

A Citadel Press Book
Published by Carol Publishing Group
Citadel Press is a registered trademark of Carol Communications, Inc.
Editorial Offices: 600 Madison Avenue, New York, N.Y. 10022
Sales and Distribution Offices: 120 Enterprise Avenue, Secaucus, N.J. 07094
In Canada: Canadian Manda Group, P.O. Box 920, Station U, Toronto, Ontario M8Z 5P9
Queries regarding rights and permissions should be addressed to
Carol Publishing Group, 600 Madison Avenue, New York, N.Y. 10022

Carol Publishing Group books are available at special discounts for bulk
purchases, sales promotions, fund-raising, or educational purposes.
Special editions can be created to specifications. For details, contact Special
Sales Department, Carol Publishing Group, 120 Enterprise Avenue, Secaucus, N.J. 07094

Manufactured in the United States of America

10   9   8   7   6   5   4   3   2   1

Library of Congress Cataloging-in-Publication Data
Golden, Christopher.
Sophomore slumps : disasterous second movies, albums, singles,
books, and other stuff / by Chris Golden.
p.   cm.
"A Citadel Press book."
ISBN 0-8065-1584-8
1. Sequels (Literature)—Humor.   2. Motion picture sequels—Humor.
I. Title.
PN6231.S497G651994   94-20517
700'.207—dc20   CIP

For my brother, James Laurence Golden III,
with whom I listened to most of the music,
and watched most of the movies and television
shows in this book, regardless of their artistic merit
. . . and I'd do it again!

CONTENTS

viii

Contents

Acknowledgments

Special thanks are due to my agent, Lori Perkins; my editor, Kevin McDonough (whose idea this was—and doesn't that phrase sound like Yoda?); my wife, Connie Golden; Stephen R. Bissette; Melissa Tapply; Steve and Patty Williams; *Billboard* magazine; Exhibitor Relations Inc.; and Jerry Ohlinger's Movie Material Store.

INTRODUCTION

The bigger they are . . . well, you know the rest. The sophomore slump is a very familiar phenomenon in professional sports and has become a common reference especially in baseball. A new player has a fabulous rookie season and the second season performs miserably. Most of these players come back in later years and play very well, but some never recover from that slump.

Even the briefest of examinations will show that the sophomore slump phenomenon is not isolated within the sports industry. Corporations, nations, organizations, politicians, and others have experienced it as well. Nowhere is the sophomore slump more entertaining, however, than when illustrated by examples from the entertainment industry itself. This book shall concern itself with five specific categories, each with its own criteria of selection: movie stars, film directors, musical acts, TV stars, and authors. Though the choices for each category will be explained in the introduction to that particular section, before you jump to conclusions let me reassure you of several things.

First, this is not a book about movie sequels and television spin-offs. It concerns itself with individual celebrities rather than the success of the programs themselves (for instance, *M*A*S*H* was followed by *AfterMASH*, which bombed without Alan Alda).

Second, when looking at an individual's performance in one medium (film, TV, or music) we will discuss, but not consider, previous successes or failures in other media.

Third, with few exceptions, we don't do so-called one-hit-wonders. If a musical group, an actor, or director had one hit film, album, song, or show and then faded into oblivion, that doesn't count. This book is about failed second efforts after all.

Researching this book, I came up with literally dozens of interesting anecdotes that do not fit into the parameters of the book but that are gems all by themselves, including the early TV appearances that movie stars like Wesley Snipes and Michelle Pfeiffer would love us to forget. Others, like Sylvester Stallone's first starring role (it's not what you think!), the "lost" Clint Eastwood film, and David Letterman's secret shame, have all snuck in somewhere.

Sophomore Slumps is a book about huge success followed by often crippling failure, about people and groups who rocketed to stardom, then faltered at the second stage. Some sophomore slumps were merely setbacks. Others meant complete obscurity at best, financial ruin at worst.

Here, together for the first time, are dozens of stories, painful and amusing, of extraordinary failure. Overnight sensations, and overnight flops. Read them a few at a time to truly savor the humiliation, embarrassment, or mere humor of each. Giggle at the tumultuous turns in the careers of your favorite celebrities. Learn something. Go and rent a movie, buy an album, watch reruns in syndication.

Nobody's perfect. That's never been more true than in the pages of this book.

Part One: Movie Stars

"You're only as big as your last picture," or so Hollywood wisdom tells us. Few actors hit it big the first time out, however. Most have to slog through dozens of forgettable roles, or create wonderful performances in forgettable films, or if they are lucky, snag small, quality roles in successful films. But there's always that one big film.

For Sylvester Stallone, it was *Rocky*. Sure, he'd made *Rebel* in 1973, *Lords of Flatbush* in 1974, *Death Race 2000* in 1975, and even *Cannonball* earlier in 1976. But it was *Rocky* that made him a star. It was a huge hit, an Academy Award winner, and Stallone was on top of the world. Then, two years later, in 1978, he released a pair of bombs, *Paradise Alley* and *F.I.S.T.* Regardless of the quality of these films, they were unqualified disasters.

But we'll get to Sly.

The criteria used for this section of the book were fairly rigid and, unfortunately, forced me to delete many actors I had originally hoped to include.

All the actors in this section were chosen because the first film in which they starred (played the main male or female character) was a major hit—and the second a huge disappointment. Ensemble films such as *The Big Chill* and *Diner* do not, as a rule, have "stars" per se and so in many cases have not been included in the weighing of eligibility for this section. Digressions are explained within the individual entries.

The definitions of hit and flop are usually financial, though not always. Some films considered hits in the following pages made significantly less money than others considered flops. It's all relative within the career of the actor in question (and the sometimes subjective opinions of the author). The film, program, or record that constitutes the slump is not always a bad one and, in many cases, is actually as good as or better than the subject's initial effort.

Sit back, relax, enjoy, make sure there's TP on the roll, and get a scratch pad so you can make a list of all the really bad movies you haven't seen.

Go ahead, I'll wait.

JENNIFER BEALS

Ah, who can forget 1983's *Flashdance*? Those of us who were of a tender, gullible age ate the film up with reckless abandon. As improbable a fantasy as it was, *Flashdance* was also a blockbuster that earned $95 million. The beautiful newcomer, Jennifer Beals, played a welder (yes, a welder for God's sake!) named Alex Owens, who dreamed of making it as a dancer. In her spare time, Alex could often be found "flashdancing" at a local club. This wasn't stripping exactly, but it wasn't any less prurient because she kept her clothes on.

Enter the tall, dark, and handsome building contractor, played by Michael Nouri, who since this hit has led a mediocre career that recently saw him playing something like eighth banana on the lame TV series *Love & War*. Nouri's character in the film, within the traditional boundaries also inhabited by Richard Gere's *Pretty Woman* lead, gets romantically involved with the down-and-out heroine and uses his money to come to her rescue. In this case, he fronts her the cash for her interview and tuition at a New York dance company.

Time was impressed by the film's success, describing it as "airheaded," among many other things. "*Flashdance* has made it big," the magazine stated in its May 9, 1983, issue, "by taking experiences of black youths and playing them in white-

From blue-collar to ripped collar—Jennifer Beals as the welder-turned-dancer from *Flashdance*.

3

face. The Flashdancers' moves can be seen any week on *Soul Train* or on any inner city street corner. But unlike its grittily romantic predecessors, *Flashdance* is pure glitz."

Director Adrian Lyne's (*Fatal Attraction*, *9½ Weeks*) second film, *Flashdance* accomplished many things. When Clark Gable went bare chested in *It Happened One Night* Hollywood legend tells us that American T-shirt sales fell off by 50 percent. With the release of *Flashdance*, women all across the nation began wearing ratty sweat shirts with the collars torn out, pulled down to bare one shoulder. It didn't last any longer than disco, and it was far less painful. Stevie Wonder's studio guitarist, Michael Sembello, became a one-hit-wonder with "Maniac," one of the songs from the film.

And, of course, Jennifer Beals became a major movie star. The Next Big Thing. Though there was a bit of controversy over who actually did the dancing attributed to Beals in the film, *Flashdance* had put her on the map and everyone was waiting to see how the diva would follow up such a mega-hit. It wasn't Thanksgiving, so nobody was expecting turkey. But that's just what we got.

James Whale's 1935 *The Bride of Frankenstein* is considered an extraordinary film. Novelist Anne Rice has called it "one of the greatest horror films ever made." It's a true classic. The mystery here is who had the brilliant idea of remaking the film for its fiftieth anniversary, starring our lovely Miss Beals as The Bride and widely respected rocker Sting as Doctor Frankenstein. It was an unqualified bomb.

Not only does the relationship between the Doctor and the Bride become a nightmarish version of *My Fair Lady*, with appropriately dramatic lighting and weather, but to afford them the luxury of the time to accomplish that, the monster, played by the talented Clancy Brown, runs off to join the circus! (Come on, I couldn't make this stuff up.) The monster, apparently wishing to allow his intended some time to rethink her initial rejection of his advances, hits the road to develop a high-wire act with his new partner, a dwarf named Rinaldo.

Though Sting later proved himself in such films as *Stormy Monday*, here he cannot avoid being perceived as foolish and as directionless as the rest of the sleepwalking cast in this laughable film. In fact, *Time* declared that "neither Sting nor Beals seems capable of full human animation," and called *The Bride* "the year's

Sting may have recovered from the howlingly awful *The Bride*, but Jennifer Beals never did. Copyright © 1985 Columbia Pictures Industries, Inc. All rights reserved.

5

most excruciatingly chichi film." (Whatever the hell "chichi" means . . . wasn't he Fonzie's cousin?) The film grossed a dismal $3.5 million at the box office.

Beals, who two years before had become the brightest new star in the Hollywood firmament practically overnight, had become a nonentity just as quickly. Unlike many of the celebrities featured in this book, Beals was never able to recover from the embarrassment of *The Bride*. Instead, she went on to make a short string of films that were, if not all bad, then certainly all eminently forgettable: *Blood and Concrete*, *Club Extinction*, *The Gamble*, *Indecency*, *Split Decisions*, and *Vampire's Kiss* went nowhere. Perhaps Beals's only other notable performance was in Shelley Duvall's Faerie Tale Theatre production of *Cinderella*, which was not released in theaters and in which she starred with Matthew Broderick.

However, don't count her out yet. Miss Beals has recently begun filming *Devil in a Blue Dress* based on Walter Mosley's mystery novel and starring Denzel Washington. If that doesn't put her star back in the heavens, nothing will.

CHEVY CHASE

Clearly the chief member of *Saturday Night Live*'s Not-Ready-For-Prime-Time Players, Chase was also the first to leave for a lucrative film career. Though he had appeared briefly in several films, including *Tunnelvision* and *The Groove*

Tube, the comedian, best known for his pratfalls, first had a lead role opposite Goldie Hawn in the 1978 espionage comedy, *Foul Play*.

Chase portrayed a goofy but lovable police detective who intends to protect, and perhaps also bed, Hawn's character, an innocent woman whom dumb luck has chosen to involve in an international conspiracy to murder the Pope. Of course, the pair fall in love, and save the Pope's life in the bargain, but not without first finding themselves in some hysterical scenes, with supporting cast member Dudley Moore as an orchestra conductor with some pretty peculiar sexual habits.

In an era that included *Heaven Can Wait* and *Oh, God!*, *Foul Play* was yet another feel-good comedy, and America was eating them for breakfast in those days. During a time of inflation, gas lines, and Jimmy Carter's "Mailaise," these films were just what the doctor ordered. And, apparently, a lot of people were following the doctor's advice.

Poor reviews (*Newsweek* said that the film's "frenetic eagerness to please is about as refreshing as the whiff of an exhaust pipe on a hot city afternoon") could not counter the fact that Chase and Hawn were both loved by American audiences for their previous work, both in film and television.

And the box office showed it. *Foul Play*, a fun little romantic comedy, earned more than $56 million, making it a certified hit in 1978, when so very few films made it to the $100 million club, and comedies even less frequently.

Knowing a good thing when they cashed their checks, Hawn and Chase would team up again two years alter for *Seems Like Old Times*. Unfortunately, before that, Chase had a sophomore slump on the way.

In 1980, Chase starred with Jane Seymour, Omar Sharif, and America's favorite dog, Benji, in *Oh, Heavenly Dog!* What they were thinking, we may never know. What we do know is that Chase was featured as a detective who is murdered and who comes back from the dead as Benji in order to solve his murder and to exact vengeance on the killers. Played as a horror film, this might have been a fun cross between *Cujo* and *The Crow*. As a kids' film, it was absurd and, even worse, badly executed. It pulled in less than $8 million.

New York Times critic Janet Maslin wrote, "*Oh Heavenly Dog* is diverting enough for its dog tricks—I like dog tricks, don't get me wrong—but it otherwise shows few signs of life." Maslin also explained that she had trouble figuring out why Chase was better as the dog than as himself. Interestingly, the film was also a slump for its canine star, whose *Benji* (1974) had been a big success.

Chevy Chase is known for humor and charm, among other endearing qualities. It has become apparent over the years, however, that without a good script and good direction, he can be boring to the point of annoyance. As previously noted, he recovered quickly from his sophomore slump by returning to the screen with Hawn in *Seems Like Old Times*, the tale of a man wrongfully arrested for robbery who turns to his ex, the wife of the district attorney

(Charles Grodin) for help. This hysterically funny film earned $40 million at the box office, instantly redeeming the actor-comedian for his, ahem, dog days.

Like *Foul Play*, *Seems Like Old Times* borrowed plenty from the classic romantic comedies of the thirties and forties and parlayed such acquisitions into real success. Critics could laugh as well as anyone, and could appreciate the performances of the cast, but both films were drubbed for being pale imitations. "*Seems Like Old Times*," wrote *Newsweek*'s Jack Kroll, "is asking for trouble in evoking the comparison [with the classic films]; this is a smart and funny movie much of the time, but it's not *that* smart and funny."

Chase has gone on to repeat this high-low cycle many times. His hits have included *Caddyshack*, *Fletch*, and the *National Lampoon's Vacation* trilogy. Among his bombs are *Caddyshack II*, *Under the Rainbow*, and the utterly awful *Deal of the Century*. His many other films range between these two poles, though most are at least enjoyable for Chase's goofiness.

In 1993, Fox launched *The Chevy Chase Show* to compete with the other boys of late night—Letterman, Leno, and Hall. Interestingly, Chase's first guest was Hawn herself. Unfortunately, like several of his films, nobody watched Chase's TV show, and Fox pulled the plug after only a few weeks, barely giving the host time to get his seat warm. Still, in a popular series of commercials for Dorito's tortilla chips, Chase rose above his misfortunes by poking fun at the show's fate. His latest release, *Cops and Robbersons*, was a flop even though the critics hated it—strange because with Chase's track record, that's generally a good sign.

Though his career has been a roller coaster both in quality and in box office dollars, one thing can most definitely be said about Chevy Chase. When he's on, he's *on*, and he is one of a kind.

GLENN CLOSE

One of the great actresses of our time, Close began her career with character roles in such films as *The Stone Boy* and *Orphan Train*. Not long after, she moved up to supporting roles in such fine films as *The Natural* and *The World According to Garp*. Finally, she had a major role in one of the defining motion pictures of the 1980s, Lawrence Kasdan's star-studded ensemble, *The Big Chill*. One thing is for certain—by the time Glenn Close got around to performing her breakout role in the 1985 blockbuster *Jagged Edge*, nobody could call her an ingenue. She was far from an overnight success.

No, Glenn Close had been working at her craft for years. And by the time the big break came along, with a script by Joe Eszterhas (whose *Basic Instinct* would later turn Sharon Stone into an international sex symbol), Close was ready for the title of "movie star." In fact, though her costar, Jeff Bridges, had already starred in several movies and a couple of bona fide hits, Close claimed top billing in *Jagged Edge*.

The film was tried-and-true Hollywood formula, prompting the *New Yorker*'s Pauline Kael, who otherwise enjoyed the film, to deem it "remarkably unimaginative." Close was Teddy Barnes, a defense attorney led by career politics to defend an alleged wife-murderer played by Bridges. Their lawyer-client relationship soon blossomed into a torrid love affair, the plausibility of which was rescued only by the audience's willingness to buy into the whole story. Of course, Bridges's character is cleared of any wrongdoing just in time for Close to discover that he is *probably* the killer after all, though like the notorious ending of Eszterhas's later film, *Basic Instinct*, the finish of *Jagged Edge* left many in the audience looking for a more concrete resolution.

Nevertheless, the performances went a long way to soothing over some unlikely plot elements, and the film made $37 million, even with Bridges playing against type. Also starring Peter Coyote and Robert Loggia, *Jagged Edge* catapulted Glenn Close past the respectable celebrity she had previously attained and straight into true stardom.

"The characters are distinctively pungent," Kael wrote, "the way they sometimes were in the thrillers of the forties. . . . Good thrillers have an electric current running through them; here it runs through Glenn Close's performance."

That same year, 1985, with the even greater success of *Fatal Attraction* still two years in the future, Close was also featured in a quirky film unlike anything she had done up to that point. An imaginative fantasy, *Maxie* featured

Glenn Close in a dual role, with Mandy Patinkin and Ruth Gordon joining the cast. Intended to be a heartwarming comedy, *Maxie* tells the story of an uptight secretary who becomes possessed by the ghost of a high-spirited 1920s flapper whose antics change her life forever.

Like *Jagged Edge*, *Maxie* is drenched in time-honored Hollywood formula, but there the comparisons cease. While the former succeeds despite its more inane moments, the latter is hysterically inept, its laughs coming for all the wrong reasons. This is one of those instances, of which you'll find many in this book, when you've just got to ask yourself, "What the heck were they thinking?"

What was Glenn Close thinking when she agreed to make a whimsical fantasy film with a director whose previous claim to fame was the Chuck Norris martial arts flick, *A Force of One*? Close had already established herself as a respectable actress, had worked with some of the best writers, directors, and performers in the business. Perhaps there was something about the goofy script for this film that appealed to her, but *Maxie* was a bad move for Glenn Close. Perhaps the saving grace of the film was that it seemed like such a turkey even in its marketing that nobody was interested in seeing it in the first place, and, therefore, nobody remembers it well enough to associate Glenn Close with a movie that awful. It earned just $2.5 million, its high point the final performance of the effervescent Ruth Gordon.

In the pages of *People*, Peter Travers was merciless. "Those who shell out good money to see this sterile, lifeless exercise in failed fantasy may find forgiving feelings hard to come by.... *Maxie* is a disaster," he wrote, "a brew of curdled whimsy chockablock with cutesy dialogue and career-crushing performances." He went on to call Close "an intelligent actress who should know better."

Perhaps, but luckily for Close, Travers was wrong about her career. The actress went on to extraordinary success in such films as *Fatal Attraction*, *Dangerous Liaisons*, and *Reversal of Fortune*. She made a name for herself on television with the Hallmark Hall of Fame production, *Sarah, Plain and Tall*, and in 1993 stormed the stage with her portrayal of Norma Desmond in Andrew Lloyd Weber's *Sunset Boulevard*. Close was so perfect for the role that Weber's people

Maxie: a role to forget for Glenn Close. © 1985 Orion Pictures Corporation. All rights reserved. Photo by Wynn Hammer.

13

paid in the seven figures to cut Patti Lupone from her contract so Close could later open the show on Broadway.

While a string of box office duds have tarnished the careers of contemporaries such as Jessica Lange and Meryl Streep, Close seems to be the Teflon actress, her career unscathed by such things as the failure of *Immediate Family* with James Woods, and her cameo in Steven Spielberg's flop, *Hook*.

REBECCA DE MORNAY

From the moment she first appeared, in Tom Cruise's living room in *Risky Business*, Rebecca De Mornay was a star. She had the same effect on millions of teenage boys as she had on Cruise's character in the film . . . love at first sight.

In the 1983 film, Cruise plays Joel, a sexually frustrated suburban Chicago teenager whose friends are all excited because his parents are going out of town. It isn't long before he's making love all over the house with a prostitute named Lana (De Mornay), whom he can't afford to pay. From there it's only a hop, skip, and a jump to Joel turning his parents' home into a whorehouse for several days, and turning a tidy profit. Of course, it's not quite that simple, but it is funny and very, very sexy. In fact, so is De Mornay. Her character is not what you would expect. She's soft-but-plainspoken, intelligent, and powerful, and De Mornay's comic timing is all but perfect.

Though *Risky Business*, which *Newsweek* called "fresh, hypnotic and very sexy," and which earned $63.5 million, is the film that made Tom Cruise a star, it also began De Mornay's career with a considerable head start. She more than held her own with the burgeoning international superstar, and so directors and producers sought her out for good reason.

But, whether brought on by bad choices or bad results, De Mornay's career was preparing to suffer some nearly fatal errors. In 1985's *The Slugger's Wife*, a real snoozer from Neil Simon, De Mornay plays a woman who falls for an egocentric baseball player (Michael O'Keefe). The film went nowhere, pulling in a paltry $3 million.

Newsweek's David Ansen trashed the film, calling it "an example of creative anorexia: the movie is so thin you leave the theater feeling you've watched the outtakes by mistake.... Martin Ritt steals a couple of scenes as the team's opportunistic manager. But with forgettable scenes like these, there's nothing grand about the larceny. Better someone had stolen the whole script and hidden it."

Though De Mornay's next effort, the Eric Roberts/

The Slugger's Wife started a string of disappointing films for Rebecca De Mornay, seen here with Michael O'Keefe. *All rights reserved. Copyright © by Warner Bros. Inc.*

Jon Voight starrer *Runaway Train*, directed by Andrei Konchalovsky, was a big hit with critics, it was also a big box office disappointment, barely scraping past $6 million. Though seemingly aware that it was not what audiences wanted, *Time*'s Richard Schickel still championed the film, calling it a "weirdly compelling movie that is an act of either high creative courage or heedless self-destructiveness," and seemed to think that either was equally admirable.

De Mornay continued to make such films as *And God Created Woman*, *Feds*, and *Pecos Bill, King of the Cowboys* which died right out of the gate. Only her acclaimed supporting performance in *The Trip to Bountiful*, for which star Geraldine Page received the Oscar, relieved her slump, though not financially.

Finally, in the early nineties, De Mornay's career turned around. A small part in Ron Howard's *Backdraft* and the lead role in the sleeper hit, *The Hand That Rocks the Cradle*, De Mornay's biggest moneymaker ever, including *Risky Business*, made her a hot property once again. Keeping in mind the mediocre performance of *Guilty as Sin*, in which she starred with Don Johnson, we can only wait and see whether she will be able to capitalize on her resurrected career.

LOUISE FLETCHER

"The curse of Oscar," they call it. Frequently in the history of Hollywood, when a talented newcomer has received an Academy Award, that actor or actress has been summarily swallowed up by a black hole and never done anything of substance again. It's a bit of an exaggeration in most cases, but, sadly, not in the case of Louise Fletcher.

Her previous credits included some TV work and a supporting role in a long-forgotten film, *Russian Roulette*, starring George Segal. And yet her lack of experience didn't stop director Milos Forman from giving Fletcher the role of her life, as the cruel, evil, sadistic Nurse Ratched in *One Flew Over the Cuckoo's Nest*.

The film, based on the novel by Ken Kesey, featured Jack Nicholson as R. P. McMurphy, an uppity convict whose bad behavior and pretense of insanity has caused him to be remanded to an asylum for observation. That's where Fletcher comes in. Her character rides herd over the patients at the "hospital," an all-star cast of what McMurphy calls "mental defectives," including Christopher Lloyd, Danny DeVito, Brad Dourif, and Will Sampson, a challenging role for any actress, and especially one as untried on film as Fletcher.

Fletcher's performance is a marvel, a ballet of human cruelty. She calmly explains why she will not give Mr. Cheswick his cigarettes, smugly defuses McMurphy's attempt to watch the World Series, and, knowing he is completely sane, she suggests the hospital keep him committed. In these scenes the sadist smoldering in her eyes, and the lines of her face, speak volumes. When Nurse Ratched's vile manipulations drive Billy Babbitt (Brad Dourif) to suicide, the pleasure she takes in his humiliation is truly unsettling.

And then of course there was Nicholson. Like Nurse Ratched, who was able to overcome the charm, the presence of McMurphy, Fletcher succeeded in doing the near impossible for a rookie—holding her own with Jack Nicholson. To the patients in the "Cuckoo's Nest," Nurse Ratched was the living embodiment of evil. *Newsweek*'s Jack Kroll said at the time that Fletcher turned "impassive coolness into a destructive force." A total bitch. And Oscar loved her for it.

In 1975, *One Flew Over the Cuckoo's Nest* won the five major Academy Awards, for Best Picture, Director, Screenplay, Actor, and Actress, an achievement reached by only two other films in Hollywood's history (*It Happened One Night*, with Clark Gable and Claudette Colbert, in 1934, and *The Silence of the Lambs*, with Jodie Foster and Anthony Hopkins, in 1991). It earned more than $133 million, losing the number one spot for the year to a little fish story called *Jaws*. Louise Fletcher had to have been stunned by her sudden fame and accolades.

Perhaps that explains the choice she made for her next big film project. Maybe, thinking back on the $165 million success of *The Exorcist* in 1973, she didn't even read the script for *Exorcist II: The Heretic*. Maybe the attraction of working with actors the caliber of Richard Burton, Max Von Sydow, and James Earl Jones was greater than the need to find good material. Whatever her reasons, Louise Fletcher made what turned out to be a fatal error when she took part in the creation of *Exorcist II: The Heretic*, widely regarded as the cinematic equivalent of a "bad trip." As the doctor experimenting on Linda Blair, Fletcher is one of the few bright spots in a story so vague and muddied it becomes nearly opaque.

Picking up very loosely after the blockbuster original, *The Heretic* is 110 minutes of jumbled nonsense, of visions and melodramatic music, of bad acting and bad karma. If there's any justice in the world, director John Boorman, who had proven himself quite a talent with *Deliverance* and *Hell in the Pacific*, is still losing sleep over this film, a major financial disaster for Warner Brothers, earning only $28 million, a far cry from the original's blockbuster status.

"It's funny," *Newsweek*'s Kroll wrote in 1977, "how these demons can blast a townhouse to smithereens but can't put the kibosh on one adolescent girl."

Or maybe it wasn't that funny.

While the other cast members were not so unfortunate, Louise Fletcher's career was, for all intents and purposes, over after *Exorcist II* was

Nurse Ratched's wretched string of flops started with the dubious sequel *Exorcist II: The Heretic.* Copyright © by Warner Bros. Inc.

19

released. She went on, first, to supporting roles in such films as *The Cheap Detective* with Peter Falk and *Brainstorm*, and later was pretty much relegated to low-budget genre fare with titles like *Mama Dracula*, *Strange Invaders*, and *Shadowzone*, as well as more upscale failures, including *Blue Steel*, V. C. Andrews's *Flowers in the Attic*, and the 1986 remake, *Invaders From Mars*.

EDWARD FURLONG

20

It was an old-time Hollywood "discovery," or at least that's what the publicists wanted us to believe. According to them, Eddie Furlong was spotted on the mean streets of L.A. and handpicked by the producers to play John Connor, the character around whom the mega-blockbuster *Terminator 2: Judgment Day* ostensibly revolves.

Connor, conceived during a love scene between Michael Biehn and Linda Hamilton in the original *Terminator*, is fated to grow up to be the savior of mankind in its last battle with thinking machines that will by then have taken over the world. The original film saw a future cyborg (Arnold Schwarzenegger) sent back in time to eliminate Connor's mother before he was born. Biehn's character, also from the future, not only prevented the cyborg from completing its duties, but, ironically, fathered John Connor.

Big shoes for a young actor to stop into, especially with the financial expectations weighing on *Terminator 2*, a film that cost ten times more to make than many films earn. Still, Furlong performed admirably. If the publicists are to be believed, it was not much of a stretch for the young actor. A wisecracking kid from the streets of L.A., being paid to virtually play himself, albeit in extraordinary circumstances, Furlong exudes a natural charm in the film and is able to tear the audience's attention away from the special effects, the leading man, and even from Linda Hamilton's newly muscled physique for a time.

And, of course, the movie hit with extraordinary financial precision. Nearly $205 million later, producers were still counting their money from overseas, cable, and video.

The kid's good. He's in position to become the Next Big Thing. And then, somehow, someway, his agents, managers, all the people responsible for his blossoming career (which is a custody nightmare we'll not go into here) let him sign up to do *Pet Sematary II*. Sing along folks, you know the song by now . . . "What were they thinking?"

Pet Sematary is a novel of black magic and obsession. As written by Stephen King, it is a terrifying tale of what happens when humanity dabbles in the unknown. The film version, with a wonderful performance by Fred Gwynne, was quite faithful to the book (with the exception of a single, added sound effect at the end that defuses the novel's great ending) and was difficult to watch. Repulsive to a fault, unsettling, frightening, and even at times darkly comic, *Pet Sematary* was not a great film—critics despised it—but it was good just the same.

The first film had a closure that told the audience the story was over. There was no room for a sequel. That should have been the first warning to Furlong and his representatives that something was wrong with this picture, literally. Second, the characters are inestimably dumb, and therefore unbelievable, and that had to have been clear from merely reading the screenplay. Finally, the first film earned a couple of bucks, but it wasn't a big hit. There was simply no reason for Furlong to make this film, but he did.

The two films tell the story of an ancient Indian burial ground that will give new life to dead things buried there. In the first movie, a whole family is destroyed by their connection to the cemetery. In the second film, even after seeing a pet and a person, resurrected by the place's magic, become homicidal lunatics, Furlong still wants to bury his dead mother there. There is a certain ironic parallel between the stupidity of that choice by Furlong's character and the stupidity of the actor himself in choosing the role at all.

"Like its progenitor," *People*'s Ralph Novak said, "this movie is consistently repulsive. It would be criminal to let anyone under 11 see either film."

Needless to say, *Pet Sematary II* flopped miserably, pulling in $17 million. While not receiving a wide theatrical release, Furlong's next effort,

American Heart, starring Jeff Bridges, was fairly well reviewed by critics and must be perceived, especially after the debacle of *Pet Sematary II* to be a success for Furlong. In 1993, the young actor appeared in *A Home of Our Own* with Oscar-winner Kathy Bates, and in 1994, in a well-marketed sci-fi horror effort called *Brainscan*, which managed less than $2 million in its telling opening week, then disappeared.

The most interesting thing about *Brainscan* is that it would likely have gone directly to home video without Furlong as its star. As such, though he has yet to have another hit, Hollywood producers still seem enchanted by Edward Furlong.

Edward Furlong probably wishes he could bury the prints of *Pet Sematary II*. © 1992 Paramount Pictures.

⌒

INTERLUDE:

Mystic Pizza: The Shrinking Pie

When *Mystic Pizza* first hit theaters in 1988, it was nothing more than a pleasant little-girls-coming-of-age film with three unknown female stars.

But there was more going on in *Mystic Pizza* than anyone knew, and it quickly became a sleeper hit, drawing rave reviews and building up a box office tally of $16.5 million, respectable especially for a film with no major male roles, at a time when the importance of the female moviegoing audience was sorely underrated. There was talk of a TV series, which never materialized, and the film's stars were getting a lot of attention.

In *Video Magazine*, Jami Bernard wrote, "*Mystic Pizza* is as satisfying as a pie with everything on it. Each member of the marvelous trio has personality, spunk and the ability to withstand a sea-change on her way to adulthood."

And yet, one of the three women was getting far more than her fair share, and soon enough, *Mystic Pizza* would cease to be remembered for its own merits, story line, and accomplishments and would become, simply, Julia Roberts's first lead role in a feature film. Roberts, of course, would go on to become the highest-paid actress in the world. Though she had previously had a supporting role in a turkey of a film called *Satisfaction*, about an all-girl rock and roll band led by *Family Ties'* Justine Bateman, *Mystic Pizza* was Roberts's first starring role, leading quickly to *Steel Magnolias*, *Flatliners*, *Sleeping With the Enemy*, *Pretty Woman*, *The Pelican Brief*, and her one true flop, *Dying Young*.

But what ever happened to Lili Taylor and Annabeth Gish, the other two actresses whose big break came in *Mystic Pizza*? The answer, truthfully, is not much.

ANNABETH GISH

Gish had had supporting roles in two films, the moronic *Hiding Out* starring Jon Cryer, and *Desert Bloom* with Jon Voight. Neither one had featured her prominently, and neither one spent

Three ladies and a pizza. Julia Roberts, Lili Taylor, and Annabeth Gish all starred in *Mystic Pizza*, but only Roberts has driven that vehicle to stardom. Copyright © 1988 The Samuel Goldwyn Co.

any real time at the box office. And then came *Mystic Pizza*. The film concerns two sisters and their friend, all of whom work at a pizza shop in their hometown of Mystic, Connecticut, as they struggle with family, friendships, and impending adulthood.

With the cachet from having starred in the hot movie of the moment, Gish should have been well on her way to a prosperous film career. In truth, or so it seems at this point, she was near the end. In 1989, the year after *Mystic Pizza* was released, Gish appeared in *Shag—The Movie!* with Bridget Fonda and Phoebe Cates. Another coming-of-age story, this time set in the sixties, the film literally vanished from distribution in no time at all, regardless of good reviews, including Ralph Novak's comments in *People*, in which he called the film "a sweet summer breeze of a movie."

Though it picked up $5.5 million at the box office, soon the only people who remembered *Shag* were the people who made the film. Fonda and Cates would team up later for *Bodies, Rest & Motion*, but Gish, at this writing, has not had a significant role in any motion picture since that time.

LILI TAYLOR

With her quirky looks and comic timing, Taylor seemed to be a natural success story. She followed *Mystic Pizza* with a winning performance in a minor role in *Say Anything* with John Cusack, but lead roles did not seem to be forthcoming. Two years later, in 1991, she starred in two films, *Bright Angel* with Dermot Mulroney and *Dogfight* with the late River Phoenix. Both films were nonperformers, disappearing almost before anyone could have seen them. Though by all accounts good films, Taylor's second and third starring roles were D.O.A.

By 1992, Taylor was back to supporting roles, like the one she plays in *Watch It*, with Peter Gallagher. Though her humor, charm, and talent are at least equal to those of superstar Roberts's, their careers could not be more different.

Could Julia Roberts's success have had a negative impact on the career potential of Annabeth Gish and Lili Taylor, talented actresses who just happened to play similar characters in a film together back in 1988? A definite possibility. For after all, there's room for only one Julia Roberts in the world.

WHOOPI GOLDBERG

Caryn Johnson changed her name to facilitate her comedy career, and it worked. Whoopi Goldberg paid her dues on the comedy circuit, and her name was fairly well-known in certain circles long before Steven Spielberg cast her in her first film role. Many Hollywood insiders criticized the choice of Goldberg to star as Miss Celie in the screen version of Alice Walker's Pulitzer Price–winning novel, *The Color Purple*. When the film was released in 1985, the critics were silenced.

The film, which earned $94 million, recounted the life of Miss Celie, played by Goldberg, who lived hard and was mistreated for most of her days. The film earned eleven Academy Award nominations, including one for first-time actress Whoopi Goldberg, and one for a little-known talk show host named Oprah Winfrey, who had a supporting role in the film. Surprising were the lack of nominations for Danny Glover, and for director Steven Spielberg. The omission of Spielberg created quite a controversy in Hollywood, even more so when, on Oscar night, *The Color Purple* did not win a single award.

In any case, it was a triumph for Goldberg. The nomination was but the icing on a cake that included working with the most respected names in several industries. But then Goldberg faced the same problem dealt with by all the celebrities included in this book. What next? How to follow up such an incredible year?

Unfortunately, there has always been a dearth of strong dramatic roles for women, and even more so for black women, at least in major features. On the other hand, Goldberg had already made her name in comedy and had a built-in audience there. It only made sense for her to turn toward humor as a way to further enhance her status as an actress, to broaden her fan base. And thus began a long, painful slide into one of the most notorious sophomore slumps in decades.

Some may argue that Goldberg's second film, the mediocre but likable *Jumpin' Jack Flash*, which earned $25 million, ought to be considered a success. Standing alone, it would be, but sandwiched between *The Color Purple* and a host of dismal failures, it must be called merely a mildly successful bridge between the two, an exception to the rule of that era in Goldberg's career.

Does it count as a sophomore slump? Probably not. Should Goldberg be in this book? Hell, it's my book, ain't it? Seriously, though, Goldberg is not a classic example of sophomore slump, yet the events described above do certainly make her early career worthy of note within the framework of this book.

Jumpin' Jack Flash sounded like a good idea at the time. The comedy was about a computer operator, bored with her job, who ends up getting herself wrapped up in international espionage and intrigue. Picking a popular song from the sixties or seventies was the trendy way to title a movie at the time, and the presence of James Belushi in the cast made the film sound doubly good. But it really wasn't.

Though *Jumpin' Jack Flash* is far from Whoopi Goldberg's worst movie, and though it wasn't a complete bomb at the theaters, it was a major failure for her in light of the notoriety she gained with *The Color Purple*. The film was harmless enough to have done little damage to Goldberg's career—if she had not kept making even worse films, one after another.

Though her comedy career continued to be prosperous, leading to her cohost *Comic Relief* six times with Billy Crystal and Robin Williams, and finally, now, to her hosting the Academy Awards in 1994, Goldberg could not seem to sign on to a film that worked. Her agents and managers must have been pulling their hair out, and it is a wonder they were not all fired, as Whoopi made bomb after bomb, with films like *Burglar*, *Fatal Beauty*, *The Telephone*, *Kiss Shot*, *Homer & Eddie*, *Long Walk Home*, and *Clara's Heart*, some of which were well received by critics, but still managed to turn up nothing at the box office.

And then came *Ghost*. The same way *Pretty Woman* had rescued the floundering career of Richard Gere, *Ghost* literally picked up and dusted off the dying careers of all three of its stars, Patrick Swayze, Demi Moore, and, of course, Whoopi Goldberg. Goldberg's performance was, perhaps, the best in the film, a hysterical turn as a fraudulent psychic medium who discovers that maybe she isn't such a fraud after all.

And with that streak of bad luck broken, Goldberg was on a roll. Not long after *Ghost* came another mega-hit, *Sister Act*, then a moderately successful film with TV star Ted Danson, *Made in America*, and finally, *Sister Act 2*. One has to wonder if it was luck after all, or whether Goldberg did actually go out and find new representation. Whatever its origin, the change in her fortune has made her one of the highest-paid actresses in the world.

JENNIFER GREY

At this point, many people would probably rather sit through a double feature of *Hudson Hawk* and *Ishtar* than hear the song "(I've Had) The Time of My Life" one more time. And yet, in the context of its cinematic origin, the film *Dirty Dancing*, it isn't quite so annoying. Not quite. As *Time's* Richard Schickel said, "The rough energy of the film's song and dance does carry one along, past the whispered doubts of better judgment."

Dirty Dancing starred hunk-of-the-moment Patrick Swayze as a dance instructor at a 1960s Catskills summer resort. When he starts giving lessons in both vertical and horizontal dirty dancing to the daughter of wealthy resort guests, trouble starts. Jennifer Grey starred as the daughter, repulsively called "Baby" throughout the film.

A generally amusing film with catty women, obnoxious rich people, and, well, dirty dancing, the movie follows that triumph-over-adversity formula so perfected in *Rocky*, *The Karate Kid*, and many more. It succeeded in spawning any number of imitations, especially in the wake of the invasion of America by the dance known as Lambada, which lasted about a disco heartbeat before disappearing. Films like *Lambada* and *The Forbidden Dance* were thematic sequels to *Dirty Dancing*, but were total turkeys. Rumors of a *Dirty Dancing 2* disappeared in the rubble of the collapse of Vestron Pictures.

Though Swayze was charming in the film, it would not have worked at all were it not for the funny, tremendously enjoyable performance by Grey. Her largest prior role was in the previous year's *Ferris Bueller's Day Off*. Grey played Matthew Broderick's goody-two-shoes sister, angry at his ability to get away with anything. The role certainly gained her some attention, showcasing her comic timing and sheer talent. But the role, as mentioned, was quite small. So it was a big change for her to take the lead in *Dirty Dancing*, but it paid off for both Grey and the studio when the film earned $63 million at the box office.

(On a side note, it is fascinating to discover that, like many successful Hollywood films, a TV series was spun off from the film *Dirty Dancing*. With perennial TV flop star McLean Stevenson as Baby's dad, the TV series was a colossal bomb, lasting only three months on CBS.)

Strangely, Grey fared little better than that TV spin-off in her future projects. In some ways reminiscent of the mishandled fame of Jennifer Beals several years before, Grey made truly poor choices for her follow-ups to *Dirty Dancing*. With hindsight, it is easy to see that a sequel would have been her best bet, but further, just about any commercial project would have been better for her career than the films she did make.

The first film Grey made, as a strategic follow-up to the blockbuster success of *Dirty Dancing*, was a boring period comedy based on stories by Damon Runyon, called *Bloodhounds of Broadway*. Here we go again, you think? You're right, of course.

What Were They Thinking?

Bloodhounds of Broadway was written and directed by Howard Brookner, a screenwriter who had apparently never directed a feature film before and, in the interest of justice, never has since. The film starred a host of actors who, though well-known, had never had a lead role in an actual hit movie. Madonna, Rutger Hauer, Matt Dillon, and Randy Quaid were among them. Though these seasoned pros had been in a lot more movies than Jennifer Grey, she was the one with the highest audience expectations, the one with the most to lose.

Put this dog to sleep! Madonna and Jennifer Grey in *Bloodhounds of Broadway.*

And lose she did. *Bloodhounds of Broadway* earned less than $100,000 at the box office and was gone from the theaters faster than *Howard the Duck*. To add insult to injury, though Grey was listed second (after Madonna) in the film's credits, Vincent Canby's review in the *New York Times* did not even mention her, though he singles out nine actors whose names appeared after Grey's credit. Ah, the sins of omission!

Grey followed *Bloodhounds of Broadway* with two more invisible films, both of which had good casts but nothing else. *Criminal Justice* also starred Forest Whitaker and Rosie Perez, and the snoozy fantasy *Stroke of Midnight* had Rob Lowe at the top of its bill. Nevertheless, after those three films, Grey's career appeared to have stopped short.

Her most recent attempt to resuscitate her quickly fading celebrity came with *Wind*. Grey co-starred in the film about America's Cup sailing with Matthew Modine, whose career also badly needed a boost. The film was marketed well and had snappy advertising and an apparently big production budget. It looked good, had all the ingredients of at least a modest hit.

But nobody went.

TOM HULCE

It's impossible to forget the infantile giggle and petulant pout of Wolfgang Amadeus Mozart, as brilliantly portrayed by Tom Hulce. He is at once amusing, charming, and repellent. Hulce had a familiar face already, due to supporting roles in several films. First, in *National Lampoon's Animal House*, he played the naive "Pinto," whose efforts to lose his virginity are one of the film's *raisons d'etre*. Then he appeared in the mediocre *September 30, 1955*, a film about the effect of James Dean's death on the youth of the day, with (God forgive us!) *The Waltons'* John Boy, Richard Thomas. Finally, he appeared in a bizarre 1980 musical called *Those Lips, Those Eyes*, which featured an eclectic cast, including Frank Langella (fresh off *Dracula* the previous year), Jerry Stiller, and Kevin McCarthy.

It was four more years before Hulce would star in the title role of the film version of Peter Shaffer's play, *Amadeus*. Darkly comic and achingly sad, the film tells the tale of Mozart's life from the perspective of his greatest competitor, composer Antonio Salieri (portrayed by F. Murray Abraham, who won the Oscar for Best Actor for the role). While much of the drama is Abraham's, later portions of the film show Hulce's talent for heartwrenching pathos. It is a virtuoso performance that, if not confronted by Abraham's, might have been honored with an Oscar.

Mozart is a brat, a rightfully arrogant pipsqueak who likes to party far too much and doesn't care who he insults. He ignores his father's wishes and lustily pursues women. His ways lead him to a death devoid of dignity and the burial of a pauper. In his death scene, dictating his final work to Salieri, whom he'd long considered a friend, completely ignorant of the man's hate for him, Hulce is absolutely, incontestably brilliant.

"In a daring, powerful performance," wrote *Time*'s Richard Corliss, "this boy with the map of White Water, Wis. stamped on his face [Hulce] soon convinces the viewer that he is the pagan saint of classical music."

Amadeus was the role of a lifetime.

Unfortunately.

Due to this new perception of Hulce's abilities, he spent the next several years pursuing smaller, independent films, what we like to call "art house pictures." Some might not have intended to play that small, but did not get the attention their producers had hoped for. Others were never meant for larger audiences. These films must still be judged for their merit, and for their box office, and those that Hulce made were widely variant in quality.

The actor's first post-*Amadeus* film was *Echo Park*, a quirky but ultimately pointless film about young people striving to make it in show business. This 1986 release, set in a not very glamorous L.A. neighborhood (*Melrose Place* this ain't), also stars Susan Dey and, of all people, Cheech Marin, who just hasn't been the same since he stopped making movies with Tommy Chong. Even more interesting is the appearance here of actress Cassandra Peterson, better known to the world as Elvira, Mistress of the Dark. Though it was obviously never intended for mass audiences, and though many critics enjoyed it, *Echo Park* missed the mark even with its limited release, never gaining the word of mouth that drives so many such films to success. While *Amadeus* had earned $47 million, *Echo Park* barely squeaked out $700,000.

Hulce's 1987 thriller, *SlamDance*, developed somewhat of a following, especially in its video release, and featured Mary Elizabeth Mastrantonio and Virginia Madsen with Hulce. Though the fame he had once found with *Amadeus* has escaped him, the actor has fortunately continued to appear in small, engaging films that have been, if not embraced, at least acknowledged by critics.

In 1988, he starred in *Dominick & Eugene*, with Ray Liotta and Jamie Lee Curtis. Hulce's one recent mainstream success came in a supporting role in Ron Howard's enormously popular film *Parenthood*, which starred Steve Martin and Mary Steenburgen. Hulce followed that with two films in 1991: an interesting thriller called *Black Rainbow*, which starred Rosanna Arquette and Jason Robards, and a dark drama, filmed entirely on location in the Kremlin, called *The Inner Circle*.

Before *Amadeus*, it was hard for many people to imagine Tom Hulce as anyone but Pinto from *Animal House*. Strangely, playing Mozart so well may have hurt Hulce's career, preventing casting directors from seeing him as anyone else.

OLIVIA HUSSEY

Hussey was a true ingenue, a girl of merely fifteen when she appeared in Franco Zeffirelli's 1968 version of what many consider to be the greatest tragedy of all time, William Shakespeare's *Romeo & Juliet*. The story, about an honor-feud between two Italian families, the Montagues and the Capulets, and the romance that blossoms between the youngest children of those two families, is one of the world's most familiar. With a tragic series of events leading to the deaths of both main characters, the play's ending is decidedly un-Hollywood. But, though Zeffirelli made several changes to Shakespeare's original, it would have been considered sacrilegious for him to alter the devastating finish.

Hussey's age and that of her seventeen-year-old Romeo, Leonard Whiting, were faithful to Shakespeare's play, a first for filmed versions of the story. Still, that didn't stop Zeffirelli from including a controversial, though tasteful, nude scene in the PG-rated film. Though it was far from the first, and *West Side Story*, a musical made seven years earlier, was considered a modern version of the *Romeo & Juliet* story, Zeffirelli's film was the most successful "straight" interpretation of the classic ever made, and that despite the changes. *Romeo & Juliet* earned almost $40 million.

Olivia Hussey charmed the hearts of the public and critics alike. Her sweet sincerity, her beauty, and the tragedy of the tale served to make her Hollywood's darling for a year.

"Just one look at the wide-eyed yearnings of Olivia Hussey, 16, for Leonard Whiting, 17," read the *Newsweek* review, "is to know what Shakespeare meant when he wrote about Juliet: 'She doth teach the torches to burn bright.'"

Big things were expected in the future for Hussey and her costar, Whiting, who, appeared in *Royal Hunt of the Sun*, the following year, and *Franken-*

stein: The True Story, a television movie for NBC, and then, strangely, disappeared completely. Hussey, on the other hand, continues to make films to this day. Though some of them have been well received by critics, none have been successful at the box office.

Hussey's second film, following the incredible success of *Romeo & Juliet* and her position as a media darling, ought to have cemented her fame and set her up for the career all the critics expected her to have.

But that didn't happen.

Instead, Hussey was out of circulation for a couple of years, and next surfaced in a film of such inescapable stupidity that, in truth, the best that can be said about it is that is has a couple of fun martial arts fight scenes. The year was 1971, and the film was a major turkey, appropriately called *H-Bomb*. So disappointing were the box office results for the film that Exhibitor Relations, the company that keeps track of such things, cannot even find a record of its performance.

And that was only the beginning of the talented Hussey's slide into the oblivion of hack directors and hackneyed films. If that wasn't enough, she followed *H-Bomb* by working once again with her costar on that film, Chris Mitchum, in the 1972, slightly twisted action thriller, *The Summertime Killer*. It is actually a better film than *H-Bomb*, but then, how could it not be?

Both films beg the question. You know, *the* question.

What were they thinking?!?!?!

Somewhat better, yet no more successful, was Hussey's 1975 horror film, *Black Christmas*. A slasher film also starring Margot Kidder, it stands as somewhat of a precursor to John Carpenter's milestone, *Halloween*. A banner year in Hussey's career, on the other hand, was 1978. She appeared on television in the adaptation of John Jakes's best-seller, *The Bastard*, and in a remake of the 1927 silent classic, *The Cat and the Canary*. While the latter film made no more Hollywood waves than any of her previous efforts, it was a noble attempt at the classic *Old Dark House/And Then There Were None* formula.

From that point on, Hussey has appeared in one bad film after another, mainly of the horror, science-fiction, and thriller genres. Though she had a role in the 1982 TV miniseries remake of *Ivanhoe*, Olivia Hussey spent most of her time in films with titles like *Escape 2000*, *Virus*, and *Psycho 4: The Beginning*, all a far cry from William Shakespeare's most memorable young woman. Her latest effort, currently in production, is a horror cheapie called *The Ice Cream Man*, with Jan Michael Vincent, former baseball pro Steve Garvey, and, forgive me for the grin, Lee Majors II (not junior, mind you, but II . . . why doesn't he call himself, Lee Majors, the Sequel?).

ROB LOWE

Lowe and Andrew McCarthy, two of the earliest members of the eighties phenomenon, the "Brat Pack," each had their first major role in *Class*, a 1983 film also starring Jacqueline Bisset. Lowe is a rich preppy and McCarthy the new school chum he brings home to meet the family. When McCarthy discovers that Lowe's alcoholic mother, played by Bisset, is the woman to whom he has recently lost his virginity, the fun is just beginning. A bad film with some witty, though sophomoric, moments, it made just over $21 million. Not a blockbuster by any means, but for a film with no stars save for Bisset, who had never been a draw for the teen demographic the film was shooting for, clearly a very respectable figure.

Critics were unsurprisingly unanimous in their negative reviews, and *Newsweek's* Katrine Ames called Lowe "a pretty boy version of Farrah Fawcett, [who] gives a smirking, one-note performance."

Ouch! At the same time, the pretty boy reference was certainly accurate, and Lowe never did a thing to deny it. Instead, he made a lot of money posing for posters.

While McCarthy's next film was the relatively successful (especially on video) *Heaven Help Us*, Lowe next appeared in the screen adaptation of John Irving's novel, *Hotel New Hampshire*. It must have seemed like a brilliant move to his agents, managers, and all the people who lost the role to him. Irving's *World According to Garp* had been a sleeper hit. *Hotel New Hampshire* starred Beau Bridges and Jodie Foster, among others, and was ostensibly a drama about a family struggling to stay together in the face of tragic events. A slightly bizarre film, which may have made audiences skittish, it earned $5 million in 1984, less than a quarter of Lowe's first film . . . which had no stars!

His next effort, in which he returned to starring status, fared little better.

Oxford Blues, which co-starred Ally Sheedy and Amanda Pays, featured Lowe as an exchange student at Oxford University in England, where he attempts to win a rowing championship and get the girl at the same time. Despite a growing awareness of his name, the film earned just over $6 million. The *New York Times'* Lawrence Van Gelder was merciless. "If midtown seems suddenly aswarm with figures bent under an invisible weight," Van Gelder wrote, "they may be moviegoers taxed by the burden of credulity imposed by *Oxford Blues*."

Lowe went on to have two big hits, *St. Elmo's Fire*, the ultimate Brat Pack film, which reunited him with Sheedy, and *About Last Night*, an adaptation of David Mamet's play, "Sexual Perversity in Chicago," which costarred James Belushi, Demi Moore, and Elizabeth Perkins. In the former, he played a one-dimensional character in a world of two-dimensional people. Save for a single scene, Lowe's presence is barely noted, though he has much screen time.

The same cannot be said of *About Last Night*, perhaps Lowe's finest performance to that time. Humor and sadness abound in the film, which somehow manages to convince us that the smile we thought empty for so long actually hides a real, whole human being. It's not a perfect film, but it's the best Lowe has made.

Later films bombed in quick succession, as the bloom was off the rose for the Brat Pack. Then, in 1990, Lowe's career got a boost from his deliciously evil performance in *Bad Influence* co-starring James Spader. If the sentence, "Elvis has left the building!" means nothing to you, you must see this modern noir thriller. As a pair, *Bad Influence* and *About Last Night* define the very respectable parameters of Lowe's ability.

After a fun, small role in the blockbuster *Wayne's World*, Lowe's latest project, as of this writing, is the challenging role of Nick Andros, a deaf-mute, in the television miniseries adaptation of Stephen King's *The Stand*. Long ago having come back from his slump, the question for Lowe is, what now?

RALPH MACCHIO

First introduced to America as Jeremy on the final season (1980–1981) of TV's *Eight Is Enough*, Macchio had already had a supporting role in the 1980 feature bomb, *Up the Academy*. In 1982, he had an even smaller role in the Beau Bridges–starring prison biography, *Dangerous Company*. In 1983, he appeared as Johnny in Francis Ford Coppola's adaptation of S. E. Hinton's novel, *The Outsiders*, another supporting role, though far more high profile.

Still, it wasn't until 1984, when he portrayed Daniel LaRusso, *The Karate Kid*, that Macchio became a star. The new kid on the block, bullied by the locals and moving in on the girlfriend of the toughest guy at school, skinny Daniel needs an edge. What he finds is Mr. Miyagi (Pat Morita), a wise and funny man who trains him in the art of karate, so that he can beat his rival in a local competition. *The Karate Kid*'s formula of lovable underdog and charismatic mentor triumphing over incredible odds, kicking some tail in the bargain, raked cash in at the box office. Also starring Elisabeth Shue (*Adventures in Babysitting*), the film earned more than $90 million, a blockbuster hit at the time, and spawned three sequels (the last without Macchio).

Newsweek's Jack Kroll had tongue planted firmly in cheek when, after predicting the film would make a fortune, he wrote that *The Karate Kid* was "a piece of fantasy that may trigger a nationwide epidemic of limping little crotch-kickers."

The same year Macchio would appear in a supporting role to Nick Nolte in the film *Teachers*, but to millions of Americans, he had, in an instant, become The Karate Kid forevermore. And therein lay the problem. The next film with Macchio in the lead was a fascinating dramatic fantasy taken from the real life and American myth of guitarist Robert Johnson, the king of the Delta Blues. The 1986 film *Crossroads*, directed by Walter Hill, features Macchio as a would-be bluesman who breaks an aging musician out of an old folks home in exchange for the harmonica player (Joe Seneca) teaching him a "lost" song by Johnson, who was reputed to have sold his soul to the devil for his musical ability.

Enjoyable as it may have been, and audience members had widely varying reactions, the film was far from what Macchio's fans were hoping for in his next starring project. It grossed less than $6 million. Critics also found the film fun but uneven, with *Newsweek* labeling it "an uneasy hybrid," caught between telling its story and trying to appeal to Macchio's audience.

Lucky for Macchio, then, that he had another film ready to be released in 1986, one that would please all of his fans . . . *Karate Kid II*. Though *People* reported that the film was "ultimately too predictable, even somewhat tiresome," it still earned $115 million and snapped the actor's sophomore slump before it even had time to get started.

Macchio's film work slowed at that point, and he appeared in few films. Two, *The Karate Kid III* and the sleeper hit *My Cousin Vinny* (for which costar Marisa Tomei won the Oscar), were very successful. Others, including *Too Much Sun*, were barely noticed.

Still, he'll always be Daniel to us.

Ralph Macchio could not convince audiences he was a serious bluesman in *Crossroads.* Seen here with Joe Seneca, left, and Robert Judd, right.

MADONNA

More precisely, Madonna Louise Veronica Ciccone. Perhaps more than any other performer, Madonna defined the late 1980s. She worked hard to have the same status in the nineties, but it doesn't seem to have worked out. Madonna has apparently gone so far with her outrageous antics that she has succeeded in surpassing her audience's taste for them. We're bored now. None of this has any bearing on her live shows, which still sell out worldwide, but her album sales are down, and interest in general has long been waning. Recently, she turned off the entire hip population of America by pissing off its late night hero, David Letterman, by being nothing more than a pompous, boorish, bore.

Madonna first found fame, and the spotlight she so craves, with the release of her self-titled debut album, and its two hit singles, "Borderline" and "Lucky Star." In 1985, her album *Like a Virgin* hit a home run with the eponymous single and three other hits. If memory serves, she appeared briefly with Matthew Modine in the 1985 film *Vision Quest*, performing on stage. However, Madonna's first real film role, and her first *lead*, was in director Susan Seidelman's *Desperately Seeking Susan*.

Rosanna Arquette is a lonely housewife who lives vicariously through the sexual escapades of a woman named "Susan," whom she reads about regularly in the personals column of her newspaper. In a contrived series of events, Arquette manages to trade places with Susan, who is played with real humor and charm by Madonna, though *Newsweek*'s David Ansen wrote that she had been typecast, "and fills the bill with delightful sluttishness."

Desperately Seeking Susan was a modest box office success, earning $22 million, and was hugely popular with critics. Madonna was now much more than a singer, she was Hollywood's latest golden girl, with talent in so many areas the dollar signs must have been popping up every time her name was mentioned. And then something happened.

Shanghai Surprise with Madonna and Sean Penn quickly dispelled any illusions about Ms. Ciccone's acting abilities.

Somehow, someway, whatever acting talent Madonna obviously had simply evaporated. She is so awful in later films that it isn't hard to imagine her talent simply getting up and walking away, like one of the nine lives of a cartoon cat.

Why? Certainly Madonna would have a hard time believing such a thing could occur. She has had no trouble in holding on to her prodigious musical talents, becoming a millionaire many times over and an entrepreneur with her own corporation. Still, Madonna's later films read like a litany at a funeral for dead films. It is possible that what creative energy she had allowed for her film career was absorbed or destroyed when she married self-destructive actor-director Sean Penn in 1985. The marriage lasted only four years, while Madonna's slump continues.

And perhaps the blame does rest with Penn. Certainly he was partially responsible for the failure that followed *Desperately Seeking Susan*. In the 1986 film *Shanghai Surprise*, their first work together and her first since playing Susan, Madonna is ridiculously cast as a puritanical missionary stationed in Shanghai in 1938. A stupid premise only gets worse from there, as the film turns into a caper comedy in which its stars attempt to steal a large amount of opium. It's not hard to see why the box office total for the film was less than $2.5 million. Had their next film fared any better, *Shanghai Surprise* might be remembered as even more of a turkey than we now consider it, but it was only the beginning.

Next up, in 1987, was *Who's That Girl?* Borrowing its fundamental story from the classic *Bringing Up Baby*, the film finds Madonna leading the unfortunate Griffin Dunne on a series of misadventures. The film spawned a hit single, but otherwise has quite literally nothing in it worth mentioning. If only it had ended there, but, alas, Madonna went on to appear with Jennifer Grey in the previously mentioned atrocity, *Bloodhounds of Broadway*, which massacres several Damon Runyon stories with poor acting and direction.

Finally, in 1990, Madonna began to have a certain amount of success at the box office. *Dick Tracy*, a huge-budget adaptation of the classic Chester Gould comic strip, starred Warren Beatty and Al Pacino, and featured Madonna in the plum role of Breathless Mahoney. The film was dubiously successful making a killing at the box office, but still not living up to expectations in the wake of the performance of *Batman* the previous year. Also, though some critics actually enjoyed the film, only its makeup and effects are worth watching. Madonna is a pale imitation of forties femmes fatales.

The next year, 1991, on the other hand, brought another successful film for the singer, a documentary about her career, *Truth or Dare*. Though it did not require any acting on her part, other than what is called for in the daily life of such a pop superstar, it is actually her best film since *Desperately Seeking Susan*. In her latest attempt to become a bona fide movie star, *Body of Evidence*, Madonna plays a character whose sexual exploits reflect the singer's own well-publicized flair for the kinky. Little more than a retread of the Sharon

Stone and Michael Douglas hit, *Basic Instinct*, *Body of Evidence* also stars Willem Dafoe.

Madonna is still desperately seeking the film role that will give her the respect she seeks as an actress.

INTERLUDE

The *Star Wars* Trio

It's almost too easy. In 1977, George Lucas's *Star Wars* broke every box office record and took root in American popular consciousness forever. The most amazing thing about the success of the film was not the numbers themselves, but the fact that they were achieved with a cast of near complete unknowns. In truth, the most interesting thing anybody knew about any of the cast members was that one of them was the brother of figure skater Dorothy Hamill. Truly an uninspiring harbinger.

It didn't matter. Relying on the strength of special effects and a mythologically classic tale of good versus evil, George Lucas delivered what would become only the first of the most successful film series of all time. As these words are written, plans are under way for the second trilogy of films, to see release in 1997, 1998, and 1999. Novels and games abound; dozens of comic book series have appeared or are scheduled to appear. *Star Wars* has never been hotter.

The first film earned $322 million at the box office. *The Empire Strikes Back* pulled in $223 million, and *Return of the Jedi*, $264 million (a total of almost eight hundred million bucks, for those of you without calculators).

Newsweek's Jack Kroll wrote about *Star Wars*: "Thirty two year old George Lucas . . . has made the rarest kind of movie—it's pure sweet fun all the way. I don't know how Lucas could make so buoyant and exuberant a film, without a smudge of corrupt consciousness, in these smudged times. He says it's a movie for children—what he means is that he wants to touch the child in all of us. Only the hardest of hearts won't let George do it."

The film was the second in two years to spawn phenomenal repeat viewing. Audience members went to see *Rocky*, and the following year, *Star Wars*, not once or twice, not even four or five times, but literally dozens of times. The cash register just kept ringing, and the entire cast became superstars overnight.

The entire cast—what a strange concept when it came to this film. Four supporting characters were never seen without full body costumes. James Earl Jones lent only his voice to the role of Darth Vader. The ancient Jedi Master, Obi Wan Kenobi, was played by the venerable British star of *The Bridge on the River Kwai* and *Doctor Zhivago*, Alec Guinness. Ah, but the three principals, that was another story entirely. Who were these people?

CARRIE FISHER

Carrie Fisher, a Hollywood debutante whose parents were Eddie Fisher and Debbie Reynolds, had previously appeared only in a minor role in the ode to hairstylists, *Shampoo*, starring Warren Beatty. Here, she was the tough-talking, no-nonsense Princess Leia, a woman clearly smarter and more prepared for action than her male counterparts. A plum role for an untried actress, and yet it would be difficult to imagine anyone else playing the part.

Fisher cannot legitimately be considered to have had a sophomore slump. After all, her next leading role (after a minor part in *The Blues Brothers*) was re-creating the character of Princess Leia for *The Empire Strikes Back*. However, because she was playing the same character, it does seem fair to point out that her first post-Leia leading role was in one of the worst films of the early eighties, a bang-your-head-against-the-wall stupid turkey of a film called *Under the Rainbow*, in which Fisher starred with Chevy Chase.

Under the Rainbow, believe it or not, concerns Chase and Fisher's attempts to prevent the assassinations of a duke and duchess, amidst espionage and intrigue, in the hotel in which all the dwarf extras are staying during the filming of *The Wizard of Oz*. Say it with me now class . . . "What were they thinking?" The film earned a startling $17 million, but didn't deserve even that much. The *New York Times'* Janet Maslin wrote, "There's nothing wrong with *Under the Rainbow* that more laughs couldn't cure." And she kind of enjoyed the film!

Fisher went on to become successful in supporting roles in such films as *This Is My Life* and *When Harry Met Sally*, and found success and profit in a new field with the publication of her novels *Postcards From the Edge* and *Surrender the Pink*.

As noted, *Under the Rainbow* doesn't really count as a sophomore slump, but it is a valuable footnote when discussing Fisher's two leading men from *Star Wars*, Harrison Ford and Mark Hamill. Like the inimitable Princess Leia, the characters of Han Solo and Luke Skywalker made instant stars of the actors who portrayed them. Toys based upon them were multiplying like Tribbles in no time at all. Every kid on the face of the planet seemed to know those names. Han Solo. Luke Skywalker.

Both Chevy Chase and Carrie Fisher probably regret that they ever appeared in that tale of international intrigue and oversexed Munchkins called *Under the Rainbow*. © 1986 CBS, Inc. All rights reserved.

53

MARK HAMILL

Mark Hamill, as previously pointed out, was best known for being the brother of figure skater Dorothy Hamill, she of the salad bowl haircut and the unflatteringly named "Hamill Camel" skating maneuver. Mark seemed to have been to the same barber when he first appears in *Star Wars*, as a country bumpkin working on his uncle's farm and dreaming of flying fighter ships. In classic Hollywood fashion, his aunt and uncle are slain and he is thrust into the middle of a war, careening wildly through space with little or no guidance beyond the mysterious "Force." At the end of the film, Skywalker uses the force to pinpoint the target that will destroy the Death Star.

If only Mark Hamill had been able to use the force to find his future roles. Though rough around the edges, he was likeable enough in *Star Wars*, enough to inspire an entire generation of kids to bash each other on the head with pastel-colored plastic "lightsabers." Hamill had previously acted only in bad television movies and such and, like Fisher, was rocketed to fame along with his first big film, *Star Wars*.

Okay, let's set the stage. You're a largely untried actor whose first film role has really taken off. Kids all over the world want to be you, want to fight like you, talk like you, or if not that, then at least be your boy sidekick. So what do you do?

Well, the one thing you don't do, and Hamill did, is make a movie like

Corvette Summer. This brainless bit of shallowness might have worked as a seventies TV pilot, but as a film, it has nothing going for it. Even the presence of the to-become-talented Annie Potts is not enough to give this dog any appeal. Car chases abound in this 1978 release as Hamill goes to Vegas in search of the people who stole his 'vette. Idiocy like this was responsible for the actor losing all the steam he had built up in his feature debut (the sole reason the film pulled in the $13 million it did), but it wouldn't be long in coming back.

In 1980, *The Empire Strikes Back* returned Mark Hamill to the role that made him famous, but any hope of sustaining a career beyond the scope of George Lucas's creations had already gone out the window. The closest he came to having a hit in which he did not play Luke Skywalker came in 1981, with Lee Marvin in *The Big Red One*. The film was neither a complete success nor a total

Mark Hamill in *Corvette Summer.*
Copyright © 1978 Universal Television.

55

failure, but is still respected today. Which cannot be said of any of Hamill's other films.

They read like a litany of bad movie-making: *Slipstream*, *Black Magic Woman*, *Time Runner*, *The Guyver*, and who can forget the illustrious, Kristy MacNichol and Dennis Quaid vehicle, *The Night the Lights Went Out in Georgia*? The third *Star Wars* film again perpetuated Mark Hamill's life as a household name, but since then his only success has been as the voice of the Joker on TV's *Batman: The Animated Series*. There has been talk of Hamill playing Luke Skywalker's father, Annakin, in the new series of *Star Wars* films, but at this point, it is still only talk.

HARRISON FORD

Ford is a talented and immensely likeable actor, that is undeniable. Even so, it is incredible to think that he has starred in seven of the top twenty-five box office earners of all time (four in the top ten), not to mention half a dozen other major hits as well. At 1994's National Association of Theater Owners' ShoWest, he was named Box Office Star of the Century. The *Star Wars* series, in which he portrayed wisecracking space smuggler Han Solo, would have been enough for any other actor (certainly it was enough for Hamill and Fisher), but Ford was destined to become one of the best-loved film stars ever, period.

Hollywood myth has Ford beginning his assault on Hollywood as a carpenter, doing renovations on the homes of Tinsel Town's rich and famous. And he must have been doing something right, because long before the 1977 release of *Star Wars*, he had already worked on eight films, with some of Hollywood's up-and-coming talents. In 1973, Ford appeared in George Lucas's *American Graffiti*, and the following year in Francis Ford Coppola's *The Conversation*. Even then, he had established some of the facial expressions that would so endear him to the moviegoing public.

And of course it was Lucas who gave Ford his big break, casting him as Solo in *Star Wars*. Along with his partner Chewbacca, a huge furred alien, Han Solo turned from a life of smuggling to a noble battle to free the people of the galaxy from the Emperor's clutches. His reluctance to do that, enfused with the charm of the actor who played him, made Han Solo perhaps the most popular character of the films. He wanted money, first, and later love, and he always had a smart aleck answer for everything.

"I've got a bad feeling about this," Han Solo says in *Star Wars*, and he may have been echoing Ford's own feelings. That same year the actor had appeared in a lame made-for-TV horror movie called *The Possessed* and played second fiddle to Henry Winkler, of all people, in the film *Heroes*. *Star Wars* had really gotten the ball rolling for Ford, but he had to be very concerned with choosing his next starring role.

After taking on the Empire, Harrison Ford's fight with the Nazis seemed old hat. Seen here in *Force Ten From Navarone* with Franco Nero, Robert Shaw, Edward Fox, and Carl Weathers. Copyright © 1978 American International Pictures.

And for all intents and purposes, it was a good choice. This is not a "What were they thinking?" at all. In fact, when he was approached to star in a sequel to the Gregory Peck classic *Guns of Navarone*, with Robert Shaw, who had done *Jaws* only three years earlier, Ford must have thought it a brilliant idea. Who wouldn't? Filmgoers, apparently. Though in retrospect the film is not as bad as it is reputed to be, *Force Ten From Navarone* drew very skimpy notice from Han Solo's fans, earning only $6.5 million. It's possible that they had yet to separate character from actor. In his review, *Newsweek*'s David Ansen wrote that "Ford, required to look grim and determined throughout, hasn't decided if he's playing 'The Story of G.I. Joe,' or 'Terry and the Pirates.'"

So what is the difference between Ford and his two co-stars, who have largely disappeared from the Hollywood scene? Perhaps this: While Fisher and Hamill were biding their time, doing a bit here and there between *Star Wars* and *The Empire Strikes Back*—or perhaps simply not getting the roles—Harrison Ford was working. In 1979, he appeared in no less than four films. In two, *Apocalypse Now* and *More American Graffiti*, he had only minor roles. The other pair, *Hanover Street*, with Lesley-Anne Down, and *The Frisco Kid*, with Gene Wilder, were both enjoyable box office turkeys.

Like Hamill and Fisher, Ford's next hit was *The Empire Strikes Back*, but he had spent the time between working all over Hollywood. When it came time for L.A.'s two biggest hitters, Lucas and Steven Spielberg, to finally work together, Harrison Ford won the plum role of 1981 over other actors, including TV's Tom Selleck. The role was Indiana Jones; the movie, *Raiders of the Lost Ark* ($242 million).

And then it was one hit after another, some huge and others merely good. *Blade Runner*, underappreciated at the time, is now considered a modern classic. The list grew: *Return of the Jedi*, *Witness* ($65 million), *Indiana Jones and the Temple of Doom* ($179 million), *Working Girl* ($62 million), *Presumed Inno-*

cent ($86 million), *Indiana Jones and the Last Crusade* ($197 million), *Regarding Henry* ($43 million), *Patriot Games* ($83 million), *The Fugitive* ($180 million), *A Clear and Present Danger*, and now a fourth Indiana Jones movie is on the way. In fact, only *Frantic* and *The Mosquito Coast* actually did poorly. Quite an impressive record for a guy who started out as a carpenter. In fact, Ford recovered from his sophomore slump quite a bit better than most other victims of the phenomenon.

STEVE MARTIN

Martin had developed a sizable following through his stand-up comedy, albums, and appearances on *Saturday Night Live* long before he made the move to lead roles in feature films. The year he made that leap, 1979, he also appeared in minor roles in two of the most diverse films in theaters, The Who documentary, *The Kids Are Alright*, and, of all things, *The Muppet Movie*. But his first leading role came that year in *The Jerk*, which featured the same kind of so-stupid-it's-funny humor that had given him his celebrity . . . and boy did it work.

The incredibly goofy story had Martin starring as Navin Johnson, the son of a poor black family (you heard right!) who sets off to find his own way in the big city. Johnson is such a complete moron, and his misadventures so extraordinarily stupid, that the film does turn out to be one belly laugh after another. *The Jerk* is also notable as Martin's first pairing with Bernadette Peters, though their later joint efforts would not come near the success of this film, one of the highest grossers of 1979, pulling in an incredible $88 million.

Directed by Carl Reiner, the film is loaded with sight gags, one-liners, even tongue twisters, and when martin is finally able to find love with Peters, the laughs only get bigger. The film has been frequently compared with the best work of Jerry Lewis (by those who think that's a compliment), but looking forward to the many fine films Steve Martin would make, it seems only fair to see *The Jerk* as merely the first of those. *Newsweek*'s David Ansen

While Steve Martin and Bernadette Peters played in *Pennies From Heaven* with Rogers and Astaire–like savoir faire, audiences would have preferred *The Jerk Part II*. Copyright © 1981 Metro-Goldwyn-Mayer Film Co.

61

wrote that "if Martin ever finds the proper vehicle, he could become a first-rate screen comedian."

Prescience, or experience? In the end it didn't matter. Ansen was right.

The Jerk's success relied heavily on Martin's quirky humor and his audience's ability, essentially, to "get it." But at times, especially in his next film, Martin's humor could be too esoteric for the largest segment of his audience, teenagers. That film, *Pennies From Heaven*, which again teamed him with Peters, cost MGM a bundle to make and was an abysmal failure at the box office, pulling in only $7.5 million. The year was 1981, and Steve Martin needed to follow up his big hit with another, or at least with something his target audience would enjoy.

He didn't.

Pennies From Heaven is a dramatic-romantic-musical-comedy about the dark and dreary time of the Great Depression, adapted from a BBC miniseries. Fun stuff, eh? Well, in all honesty, yes. Despite its truly depressing subject matter and characterizations, *Pennies From Heaven* is an enjoyable film. Fans of the musical will find much to appreciate in its production numbers. No matter, however, to the filmgoers of the early eighties. They wanted the Steve Martin they knew and loved. They wanted their creativity spoon-fed to them, nice and subtly. This was too much. And it bombed.

The next starring role for Martin was, if you can believe it, even stranger, though slightly more successful in its goals. In the black-and-white film *Dead Men Don't Wear Plaid*, Martin plays a classic private eye whose investigation leads him into meetings with such Hollywood stars as Humphrey Bogart and Bette Davis, through incredible editing that allows Martin to appear along with the stars in scenes from their classic films. Weird, creative, and thoroughly enjoyable. But still not a hit like *The Jerk*.

In 1983 and 1984, Martin released two films that put him back into *Jerk* territory. Though *The Man With Two Brains* and *The Lonely Guy* weren't the kind of hits that *The Jerk* was, they were clearly more along the lines of what Martin's fundamental audience was after. The next year, 1985, brought only a minor appearance in a little-known and barely remembered film called *Movers and Shakers*, while 1986 was the year Martin teamed up with old *Saturday Night Live* pal Chevy Chase and new *SNL* star Martin Short for *Three Amigos!* A silly riff on a classic western formula, the film was a hit among kids and, well, some adults as well.

In 1987, Steve Martin starred in a film he had scripted, loosely based on the Rostand classic, *Cyrano de Bergerac*. The film was called *Roxanne*, and, with it, Martin had begun a new era for himself. Martin's screenplay was wonderfully warm and funny, and many critics and fans alike were stunned that it was not nominated for an Oscar. Nevertheless, the actor had found a new respect among his industry peers, which showed with every new step he took. In 1988

63

he starred in the moderate success, *Dirty Rotten Scoundrels*, with Michael Caine, and the following year, in the blockbuster sleeper hit, *Parenthood*, directed by Ron Howard.

Martin's one misstep in this new era was a somewhat offensive, but often funny film called *My Blue Heaven* (1990). Martin played a Mafia family member in the witness relocation program. That film did little box office business, though it would be impossible to say why. Even so, Martin more than made up for it the following year, when he appeared in three very popular films, including the remake of *Father of the Bride*, *L.A. Story*, which Martin scripted, and *Grand Canyon*, in which he played a very serious and effective role.

Most recently, in 1992, the actor was wavering. *HouseSitter*, in which he starred with Goldie Hawn, was a modest success, and *Leap of Faith* a drama with Debra Winger, was a real disappointment at the box office. Still, Martin's reputation is unscathed, and he appears unstoppable.

MIKE MYERS

Saturday Night Live has spawned an incredible number of movie stars: Chevy Chase, John Belushi, Dan Aykroyd, Bill Murray, Eddie Murphy, Billy Crystal (who didn't start there but got a huge boost from the show), Jon Lovitz, Jim Belushi, Dana Carvey, and Mike Myers. To a lesser degree, you could also include Brian Doyle-Murray, Rob Schneider, Adam Sandler, Chris Rock, Joe

Piscopo, Jane Curtin, Gilda Radner, Tim Kazurinsky, Phil Hartman, Nora Dunn, Garrett Morris, and Laraine Newman on that list. And surely there are a whole host of others we've overlooked.

But let's face it, the show has been on a gradually accelerating downhill slide since the last days of the Not-Ready-for-Prime-Time Players. In fact, in recent years, the cast has been lucky if 10 percent of the show was even mildly amusing. But once in a great while (though they later beat it to death), one of the show's cast members will hit on a genuinely hysterical character or skit. Mike Myers has done it several times, but never with as much success, or humor, as "Wayne's World."

The story of Wayne Campbell, a teenager from Aurora, Illinois, who has somehow managed to get his own show on public access cable, "Wayne's World" began as the funniest thing *SNL* had done in ages. Along with his sidekick, Garth Algar (Dana Carvey), Wayne played host to a number of special guests on his show. John Goodman played the bumbling police chief of Aurora (Myers, mumbling: "Homo says what?" Goodman: "What?"). Tom Hanks played Garth's older brother. Madonna played Wayne's greatest fantasy, and Aerosmith played themselves . . . and cranked out a new, metal version of the "Wayne's World" theme song. Even alone, Wayne and Garth were hysterical. Once again, and perhaps for the last time, people were talking about *SNL* on Monday morning.

Of course, a movie was only a matter of time, once the use of Wayne's

A career on the *Wayne*? Mike Myers (with Nancy Travis) followed up *Wayne's World* with *So I Married an Axe Murderer*, but audiences hardly noticed. Copyright © 1993 TriStar Pictures, Inc. All rights reserved.

66

favorite three-letter word, "NOT!" became ingrained in the American cultural lexicon. *Wayne's World* was a loose collection of funny gags linked together by a weak plot about the show being taken over by a sleazy network producer (Rob Lowe) and Wayne's infatuation with a singer (Tia Carrere). In truth, the best parts of the film are the goofiest, and the "Bohemian Rhapsody" segment is a priceless paean to the soul of Generation X. Wayneisms like, "sure, and later on maybe monkeys will fly out of my butt," were adopted by people across the nation. We'll leave it to you to judge the value of that phenomenon.

Wayne's World earned more than $121 million. In its first week, it had earned back 128 percent of its budget. *Newsweek*'s review was positive, claiming the film had the "knowing spirit of an old Warner Brothers cartoon. It is carelessly rambunctious, self-aware and a lot smarter than it lets on."

With the film's staggering success, a sequel was not only a natural step, but a fiscal necessity for Paramount. *Wayne's World 2* did well but didn't pull in the kind of business the first film achieved. Still, any other film would be considered a huge hit with the sequel's box office, so we'll leave it alone. And it doesn't matter anyway, because Mike Myers's sophomore slump was a completely different film.

It's been away for a while, folks, but here it comes 'round again. Myers followed the success of *Wayne's World* with a painfully dumb film called *So, I Married an Axe Murderer*. The trailer was insipid and therefore inspired little enthusiasm among audience members. One can only imagine how dumb the script had to be for the trailer to be so awful, so we've got to ask Mike Myers and his agents and manager . . . "What were you thinking?!?!"

The story of a performance artist who marries a woman he comes to believe is a murderess, the film is inexcusably stupid and only rarely elicits even a shadow of the laughter usually associated with Myers. "The definition of tepid . . . the movie does have its occasional moments," *People* said, "but they don't come often enough."

So, I Married an Axe Murderer fizzled out with frightening speed, earning a paltry $11.5 million and showing once again that there is no such thing as a sure thing. Ever. At the same time, on a related subject, the failure of *The Cone-heads* taught all of those *SNL* people a lesson, but when Hollywood still plans to release a film version of Julia Sweeney's one-joke skit, "It's Pat," and is considering a movie version of "Hans & Franz," you know the lesson is already forgotten. We can only hope that such films never get made and that, in the future, *SNL* alumni will go the route of Chase, Belushi, Aykroyd, Murray, Murphy, and Crystal, making their careers work based upon new ideas, fresh concepts.

Just because it works in a two-minute TV sketch doesn't mean it will work as a two-hour movie. *Wayne's World* is, decidedly, the exception that proves the rule.

CHRISTOPHER REEVE

An unknown at the time to all but fans of the soap opera *Love of Life*, Reeve beat out flocks of competitors (including Sly Stallone) for the dual role of a lifetime, Clark Kent and his alter ego, Superman. Taken from the comic book character, created in 1938 by Jerry Siegel and Joe Shuster, the film was certainly not the first celluloid treatment of the story, nor would it be the last. But it may well be the most successful.

As his home planet is self-destructing, little Kal-El is sent hurtling through space in an experimental ship constructed by his father Jor-El (Marlon Brando). Crashed to Earth, he is taken in by a childless couple, the Kents, and, as he grows to manhood, discovers he has extraordinary powers, superhuman abilities. As an adult, he goes to the big city, Metropolis, to become a newspaper reporter and falls for his colleague, Lois Lane (Margot Kidder). In order to perform heroic deeds without anyone recognizing him as Clark Kent, he creates the identity of Superman.

As if you didn't know. In fact, the character is one of the most recognized around the world. No wonder, then, that Reeve's first starring vehicle, at the time the most expensive movie ever made, earned more than $134 million domestically. The ad campaign claimed, "You will believe a man can fly," and for some audience members at least, they made good on their promise.

Though the popularity of the character cannot be underestimated when reporting the success of the film, it would be unfair not to also credit Reeve's talent, humor, and charisma. If anyone actually did believe a man could fly, it

Outside of his tights and cape, Christopher Reeve's career has been nothing but Kryptonite. Seen here in *Somewhere in Time*. Copyright © 1980 *Universal Pictures*.

was due in equal parts to the special effects and to the quality of Reeve's performance. Everyone could relate to him, whether as Clark or as Superman. Supporting performances by Gene Hackman and Margot Kidder also helped boost the film.

"Not since *Star Wars*," reported *Time*, "has there been such an entertaining movie for children of all ages." The same article applauded the actor's efforts, saying that "the easy authority with which Reeve handles the double role is the real surprise of the picture."

Reeve's next choice was also a romantic fantasy, though this one far more dramatic. Based on the novel by Richard Matheson, *Somewhere in Time* (1980) featured Reeve as a modern man who becomes obsessed with a long-dead stage actress and eventually must travel back in time in order to seek her love. Vastly underrated, and critically drubbed, this romantic gem features Jane Seymour and Christopher Plummer, and another charming performance by Reeve. Unfortunately, it did not reach the audience it deserved, and earned just over $9 million.

"Christopher Reeve is a very large leading man whose cartoonlike, all-American handsomeness made for an ideal Superman," wrote *Newsweek*'s David Ansen. "Here, he works very hard to prove that he is a flesh and blood mortal after all. He isn't."

As would be the case with Ralph Macchio several years later, Reeve's sophomore slump would not last long. Later in 1980, *Superman II* was released, earning $108 million, another blockbuster, though *Newsweek* called it "an amiable comic-strip flick without the aura that made the original a charming pop epic."

Unfortunately, Reeve followed *Superman II* with a long series of films that failed, many due to their boredom quotient, including: *The Aviator*, *The Bostonians*, *Monsignor*, *Deathtrap*, *Mortal Sins*, *Street Smart*, and *Switching Channels*, a supposed remake of *The Front Page* (or *His Girl Friday*, take your pick) that costarred Burt Reynolds and Kathleen Turner and was actually a poor attempt to capitalize on the recent success of *Broadcast News*. The only later Reeve film that could actually be considered successful was *Superman III* (the fourth was a major turkey).

In fact, if you discount sequels in the criteria for determining sophomore slump, then Reeve would technically still be in a slump that has lasted fifteen years.

MICKEY ROURKE

This is an unusual entry because Rourke's second starring role earned approximately three times the box office of his first. However, there are serious mitigating circumstances.

Once upon a time considered sexy for his scruffiness, Rourke managed to turn a promising film career into a source of general amusement and ridicule. In essence, the choices that the actor and his representatives have made in recent years have made him, unequivocally, the king of the what-were-they-thinking school of career planning.

But about that promising start . . . Rourke first came to America's attention in a bad television movie with Linda Hamilton called *Rape & Marriage: The Rideout Case* and a small supporting role in *Fade to Black*. That was 1980. The following year, he had a supporting role in a film that set the standard for steamy thrillers for more than a decade, *Body Heat*.

In 1982, Rourke got his first major feature film role, as the sleaziest member of a group of friends in the late 1950s in Barry Levinson's *Diner*. Rourke appeared in the ensemble cast with Steve Guttenberg, Daniel Stern, Kevin Bacon, and Ellen Barkin. Due to the nature of the ensemble, and the size of Rourke's part, it cannot be considered his first leading role, in the same way that Sylvester Stallone's first lead was not his character in *The Lords of Flatbush*. Still, *Diner* was well liked by audiences and critics, and Rourke was off to an excellent start.

The next year, 1983, was another interesting one for the actor, who had a supporting role in Francis Ford Coppola's black-and-white adaptation of S. E. Hinton's novel *Rumble Fish*. The film was a disappointment for all involved due to its no-show at the box office. But by this time, prior to his first real leading role, Rourke had already worked with some of Hollywood's greatest directors: Kasdan, Levinson, Nicolas Roeg, and Coppola.

Interestingly, it was under a director with a much quieter reputation, Stuart Rosenberg, that Rourke became the Next Big Thing. *The Pope of Greenwich Village*, based on Vincent Patrick's novel, starred Rourke and Eric Roberts (who had previously starred in *King of the Gypsies*) as cousins whose scheming gets them into trouble with both the police and the Mafia. Much attention was also afforded the film's female lead, Daryl Hannah. Though he had produced a solid body of work to that point, this film, which earned only $6.5 million, was still the one that put Mickey Rourke at the top of every casting director's most wanted list. Despite its low box office, its critical reception made it a hugely successful jumping off point for Rourke's career as a lead actor.

"Mickey Rourke is a stirring young actor with a tough poetry about him," *Newsweek* announced, "the Brando and DeNiro effect."

Heady company for a young actor, and praise that Rourke would find it difficult to live up to. In 1985, Mickey Rourke was the dashing leading man in a much-publicized film called *Year of the Dragon*, which had become highly controversial due to charges that it was racist in its treatment of Asians. The film, which concerned a cop's investigation into Chinatown gang wars, was a mishmash of films including *The Godfather* and *Chinatown*, with little originality. The female lead was an Asian model named Ariane who had less acting talent than Robby the Robot. There is not a single likeable character in the film, though John Lone makes a wonderful villain. Rourke's character is completely repulsive.

If the script and the casting of Ariane weren't enough to sound alarm bells in the actor's head, certainly someone in his employ ought to have realized that this was Michael Cimino's first film since *Heaven's Gate*, which at the time had the distinction of being the biggest disaster in the history of Hollywood. It was amazing that anyone was brave enough to hire Cimino at all, but even more amazing that an actor with so much riding on his next film chose one with him as director. Thus began Mickey Rourke's ascent into the what-were-they-thinking hall of shame.

Though *Year of the Dragon* earned more than $18.5 million, its notorious reputation and terrible reviews combined with expectations that were much higher than actual returns to the point where many believe it did actual harm to Rourke's career. Though he admitted he wouldn't mind seeing the film again, *Newsweek*'s David Ansen was particular about its many faults. In direct conflict with the same publication's claims about Rourke in his previous film, Ansen says flat out that he never believes Rourke in the role, which would have been better for "a DeNiro or a Bogart." "A lot of this over the top movie is hard to swallow," he says.

Rourke's next film is perhaps his most famous, a controversial erotic film about kink and cruelty called *9½ Weeks*, in which he starred with Kim Basinger. While discussing whether the film is good or not is almost irrelevant, it is important to note that it had a modicum of success and achieved a certain cult status.

In 1987, the actor appeared in three films. Two, the IRA-hit man-change-of-heart movie *A Prayer for the Dying*, and the Charles Bukowski auto-biography *Barfly*, were utter failures. *Barfly*, it should be noted, also starred (gulp) Frank Stallone, and let's face it, anyone trying to make a hit movie would not make it with Frank Stallone. The third Rourke film of 1987 was *Angel Heart*, a fairly successful and once again highly controversial film about a rumpled private investigator whose latest case gets him involved with voodoo and the devil, not to mention raunchy sex with *The Cosby Show*'s golden girl, Lisa Bonet.

And that was the end for Mickey Rourke. He has yet to have any amount of success, other than perhaps on video, with a film since *Angel Heart*. Though some are most assuredly better than others, and many of them feature fine, well-known actors, such Rourke films as *Homeboy*, *Johnny Handsome*, *Desperate Hours*, *White Sands*, and the absurd *Harley Davidson & the Marlboro Man* were bombs.

Even in light of those failures, we are duty-bound to report that Rourke, perhaps hoping to cash in one what remained of his following from *9½ Weeks*, made one of the worst films in years in 1990. Ostensibly an erotic drama, *Wild Orchid* also starred Jacqueline Bisset and Rourke's paramour Carré Otis, and was so awful that it almost served as a eulogy for the actor's career. It is still possible for Rourke to recover from that disaster, but unlikely.

BROOKE SHIELDS

Brooke Shields's first movie was 1977's *Holy Terror*, though many people may remember it by another name, *Communion*, or its most common title, *Alice, Sweet Alice*. Shields was ten when she made the film and appears only in its early portions, before being murdered. With the release of *Pretty Baby* in 1978, the producers of *Holy Terror* renamed and re-released their film in an attempt to capitalize on Shields's newfound success. In *Holy Terror*, she was a victim, but in *Pretty Baby* she's the star.

Famed director Louis Malle brought Shields to the American public in *Pretty Baby*, which also featured Susan Sarandon and Keith Carradine. Shields plays Violet, a young girl who has grown up in a New Orleans whorehouse. Though certainly part of the film's fame was established through the prurient interest a certain audience segment had in seeing young Brooke in such a situation, there is no escaping the quality of the film, and of the performance by the preteen Miss Shields.

Though many readers, in light of Shields's later work and her fame as a Calvin Klein jeans model, may snicker at the suggestion that Shields ever had the kind of acting talent that Malle requires of his performers, it is undeniably there. *Newsweek*'s Jack Kroll called Shields "astonishing." He went on to write, "With a hair raising, instinctive directness and spontaneity, she creates a kind of perverse Alice in Brothel-land who sees her amoral world as perfectly normal and who can't wait to take her place within it."

76

Hold up, chum. We *are* talking about the same Brooke Shields, aren't we? And yes, in fact, we are. Though there's no way you could tell that from her second starring role (she also had a supporting role in 1978's *King of the Gypsies* starring Eric Roberts), in the obscure bomb, *Tilt*. While *Pretty Baby* is still a legend, it earned only $8.5 million at the box office. *Tilt*, on the other hand, like Olivia Hussey's slump film *H-Bomb*, was so minor as to have no record of its box office income available.

The year was 1978, and the film's producers must have thought they were being hip making a movie about a young female pinball wizard. Unfortunately, the plot, what there was of it, wanders about like a staggering drunk, regardless of the presence of talented Charles Durning as Shields's villainous opponent. Other than an interesting piece of cinematography

After *Pretty Baby*, Brooke Shields moved from Louis Malle to shopping malls in *Tilt*, a pinball saga that went nowhere.

that brings the viewer inside the pinball machine, a gimmick that sounds as if it might have later shown up in a Peter Gabriel music video, *Tilt* is a completely forgettable film. And what do you know, it's forgotten.

Shields moved on to a pair of charming box office losers in 1979. First, she starred in *Wanda Nevada* with Peter Fonda, who also directed. The story of a no-account gambler and a young girl he "won" who discover a gold mine, *Wanda Nevada* also features Fonda's famous father in a cameo, the only time the two ever worked together. The second film, *Just You and Me, Kid*, starring George Burns, was a staple of cable TV for a decade. Burns is a retired vaudevillian who takes in a troubled runaway (Shields) in this heartwarming film.

Since *Pretty Baby*, Shields had not had a single hit, but in 1980 and 1981, she enjoyed her greatest success ever, with the release of *The Blue Lagoon* and *Endless Love*, two mercilessly infantile romantic fantasies that established for Shields an unfair reputation for shallowness, which persists to this day. The former film tells the story of two children, a boy and a girl, who are marooned together on a tropical island, only to grow up and, of course, mate. The latter is an overwrought tale of high school romance, directed, incredibly, by *Romeo & Juliet*'s Franco Zeffirelli. The best part about *Endless Love* was the sappy theme song by Diana Ross and Lionel Richie, which was number one on the *Billboard* charts for nine weeks.

It would be three years before Shields appeared on screen again, not a wise hiatus when one has two big hits to follow up on. In 1984, she appeared in three films. Shields had a cameo in *The Muppets Take Manhattan* and starred in two of her worst films, a lost treasure movie called *Wet Gold*, and a desert race movie called *Sahara*. At that point, it was probably wise of the still-teenage actress to announce that she was taking a sabbatical from the movie business to go to college full time.

Unfortunately, upon her return, the girl who had made every male in American want to climb into her Calvin Klein blue jeans only perpetuated more of the same. Whatever talent and charm we had glimpsed in her early work had gone right out the window somewhere along the line. With titles like *Backstreet Dreams*, *Speed Zone!* and *The Diamond Trap*, and the long-awaited flop *Brenda Starr*, Shields would probably have been better off going on to graduate school.

SYLVESTER STALLONE

Let's begin with a confession. According to the criteria by which entries for this section were chosen, Sylvester Stallone does not belong here. While most believe his first feature film lead was the title role in the blockbuster hit *Rocky*, which would make him a prime candidate, this is actually not so. Even after we have discounted his supporting or costarring roles in such films as *The Lords of Flatbush*, *Cannonball*, and *Death Race 2000*, and disqualified his appearance in the softcore *Italian Stallion*, there is still one film that ought to prevent him from being raked over the coals in this book.

In 1973, Stallone had the leading role in a long-forgotten film called

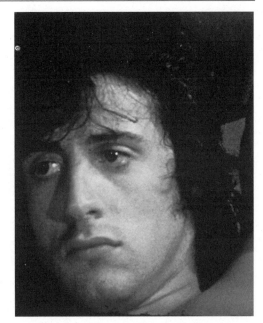

Sly Stallone in the almost never-seen *Rebel*.

Rebel. After consulting the most astute film critics I know, all but one had not only never seen the film, but never heard of it nor been aware of its existence, so limited was its release and exposure. The single authority on such films who actually knew of the film remembers having seen it at a New England drive-in about the time of its release. He seems to recall that Stallone played some kind of drifter, which doesn't gel with other reports that the film was about a politically radical student.

Due to the sheer obscurity of this film, and the possibility that it never actually received a national theatrical release, I have chosen to disqualify it. In any case, since Stallone was not only the star, but the writer of *Rocky*, this would surely be seen as his first "major" role.

Stallone had written the screenplay, and it became a hot Hollywood property, but he would not allow it to be made without him in the lead. That kind of addendum is usually a deal-breaker in Tinsel Town, but not this time. Instead, he was cast in the lead role, with veteran Burgess Meredith at his side as Mick, Rocky's manager. The film is the story of an underdog, seeking a way out of the life that has been dealt him and trying to prove to his loved ones, and himself, that he's no quitter, that he can accomplish whatever he sets out to do.

Stallone's diction left much to be desired, and his mumbling was often the butt of jokes, but thanks to the inspiring story he had written, and the $117 million the film earned, the jokes rang hollow. Meredith livened up the cast as

80

the cranky fight manager, along with Carl Weathers as the current champ, Apollo Creed, and Talia Shire as Rocky's girlfriend, Adrienne. ("Yo!")

The training sequences, in the meat-packing plant and on the streets (and stairs) of Philadelphia, have been frequently mimicked, but never with such effect as they had in *Rocky*. The theme song, "Gonna Fly Now," reached number one on the *Billboard* charts.

Rocky won the Best Picture Oscar for 1976, beating out such acclaimed films as *Taxi Driver* for the honor. "Stallone is funny, immensely likable," Jane Maslin wrote in *Newsweek*. "At heart his Rocky is that stock character—the gentle giant—but Stallone has endowed him with such vivid idiosyncrasies that the cliche takes on new life."

Years before *Hoffa*, Sly Stallone made *F.I.S.T.*, a movie about the Teamsters that got, um, buried at the box office.

Stallone cowrote the script for his second starring role, in *F.I.S.T.*, with Joe Eszterhas (*Basic Instinct*). The 1978 film is a loose and fictionalized adaptation of Jimmy Hoffa's rise to power, with Stallone as Johnny Kovak, the Hoffa-like union organizer who eventually becomes the union boss and gets in bed with the Mafia. A passable film, *F.I.S.T.* earned a fairly respectable $22 million at the box office, but in comparison with *Rocky*, and with the filmmaker's huge intentions, the film was definitely the beginning of a slump for the new star.

"A great actor might have made Johnny Kovac into an authentic tragic hero," *Newsweek* said on May 1, 1978. "Sylvester Stallone is not that actor.... Stallone charges around like a wounded bull in a political china shop, mush-mouthed, dense and fatally one-dimensional." Critics were fairly unanimous in their panning of the film and may have contributed to its shortfall.

Unfortunately, the worst was yet to come for Stallone, for the same year saw his devastatingly bad debut as a film director, for *Paradise Alley*, which he also wrote, starred in, and sang the title song for. The film, the story of three brothers struggling to get out of Hell's Kitchen post–World War II, was a bizarre mishmash of formulaic themes and earnestly goofy plot contrivances. Likely to his dismay, Armand Assante also starred in this flop, which earned $8.5 million in 1978. In its review, *Newsweek* appropriately dragged out that bull-in-a-china-shop analogy again.

The slump had become an out-of-control slide, but in 1979, Stallone arrested the downward progress with a huge career boost, *Rocky II*, the first of what would become a long line of sequels for the actor. In 1981 he made two very underrated films, the cop drama *Nighthawks* (with an incredibly evil performance by Rutger Hauer) and the World War II soccer film *Victory*, which was directed by John Huston, and starred Max Von Sydow, Michael Caine, and Pele.

1982 gave the actor two big hits, *Rocky III*, and the first in a new series (though that was not the film's intention), *First Blood*. Stallone played John Rambo, a Vietnam vet abandoned by society who is forced by the ignorance of a small town sheriff into becoming the object of a manhunt, though he ends up the hunter.

Then, in 1984, the first cracks began to show in Stallone's armor. Wanting to extend his audience beyond the adrenaline junkies who attended the Rocky and Rambo epics, the actor made *Rhinestone*, perhaps the worst film of his career. Stallone played a cab driver taken under the wing of a country diva (Dolly Parton) who vows to make him a singing star. It's no joke—you can rent it! In 1985, he returned with *Rocky IV* and *Rambo: First Blood Part II*.

And then his second real slump began. His action films *Cobra* and *Over the Top* did not become the hits they were predicted to be. *Rambo III*, which made plenty of money, was actually a failure because it was the most expensive film ever made up to that point in time. The 1989 films *Lock Up* and *Tango & Cash* were fairly enjoyable (which could not have been said of the downright awful *Cobra*), yet they also did not rake in the dough Stallone had come to be associated with. In the early nineties, the actor turned to comedy, which had never been his strong suit. The films, *Oscar* and *Stop! Or My Mom Will Shoot* were genuine flops.

Many were claiming that Stallone was washed up, his career virtually over. But the actor-director-writer-producer was not giving up so easily. He had come from far worse circumstances to get to where he was, and his intelligence and business savvy (he is one of the owners of the Planet Hollywood chain of restaurants) would bring him back to the top eventually.

In 1993, Stallone starred in two major action hits, *Cliffhanger* and *Demolition Man*, and, wanting to strike while the iron was hot, he immediately lined up a number of high-profile action films and appeared nearly naked on the cover of a national magazine. Suddenly he was not box office poison, but box office gold.

Stallone, perhaps more than any other actor, proves the old Hollywood adage that claims you're only as good as your latest film.

PATRICK SWAYZE

Swayze's first memorable appearance came in 1983's *The Outsiders*. This adaptation of the famed S. E. Hinton novel is weak in all the wrong places, considering its source material, but it is still notorious as the testing ground for an extraordinary assortment of young talent, many of whom would become superstars. The cast includes C. Thomas Howell, Matt Dillon, Ralph Macchio,

Diane Lane, Rob Lowe, Tom Cruise, Emilio Estevez, and, of course, Swayze. Interestingly enough, Howell and Swayze would move together through their next two films.

The first is a corny Cold War–pop culture classic, a guilty pleasure called *Red Dawn*. The first film to carry the PG-13 rating introduced in 1984, *Red Dawn* concerns a Communist invasion of the United States, and the actions of a small group of high school students who become resistance fighters. The film's growing paranoia is almost surreal now, but there was a time when audiences nodded knowingly as the teens executed a friend who had given them away. Also of note is a hilariously serious performance by Powers Boothe as a downed Air Force officer. When the kids ask him who's on their side, Boothe replies, "six hundred million screamin' Chinamen."

"I thought there were a billion people in China," one of the kids says naively, and you can feel the reply, and the giggle coming on.

C. Thomas Howell, Jamie Lee Curtis, and Patrick Swayze in *Grandview, U.S.A.* Copyright © 1984 CBS Fox.

"There were," Boothe says. Dramatic pause.

This film was also a roll call of young talent, with Howell and Swayze, as well as Charlie Sheen, Lea Thompson, and Jennifer Grey. *Red Dawn* was well executed and brought in a surprising $36.5 million at the box office. "Swayze," wrote John Bembrose in *MacLean's*, "convincingly communicates the emotional torment of a young man who must become a leader in a matter of hours."

The third film Swayze and Howell made together, Patrick's second leading role, *Grandview, U.S.A.*, is a coming-of-age film in which Swayze and Howell compete for the attentions of a demolition derby owner named Mike Cody, played by, believe it or not, Jamie Lee Curtis. Only three things need be said about this film. First, it is excruciatingly awful, and even more uncomfortable to watch if you are a fan of any of the three stars. Second, it died a rapid box office death, earning less than $5 million, and went unmourned. Finally, America's foremost character actress, Jennifer Jason Leigh, is also in the film, and if she has any smarts she probably leaves it off her resumé.

If proof is needed regarding the effect of *Grandview, U.S.A.* on Patrick Swayze's career, one need look no further than his next film role, in 1986. Rob Lowe was the star of *Youngblood*, the brain dead story of an aw-shucks kind of guy trying to make it in the rough and tumble world of hockey. Swayze managed to snag a supporting role in the film, but didn't seem to be going anywhere with it.

The year 1987 saw the home video release of two Swayze films that were made in some nebulous vacuum of direct-to-video space. The films, a tragic drama called *Tiger Warsaw* and a bizarre sci-fi fantasy called *Steel Dawn*, deserve mention here only in that they were released in the wake of Swayze's most successful film to that point, *Dirty Dancing*. That film made Swayze, who played sexy dance instructor Johnny, an international sex symbol and superstar. The actor, who had danced professionally, had finally found his star vehicle. Videotapes were released teaching middle-aged women how to "dirty dance," ostensibly with some promise that a young stud like Swayze would come their way.

In 1989, Swayze made two good ole boy movies, *Next of Kin*, a preposterous vigilante justice film with an inexplicably talented cast including Ben Gazzara and Sam Elliott, and *Road House*, in which he plays the new bouncer at a macho club and gives his all in an attempt to break Steven Seagal's record for most (other people's)

Patrick Swayze was a bouncer in *Road House*.
Audiences wanted more "dirty dancing."

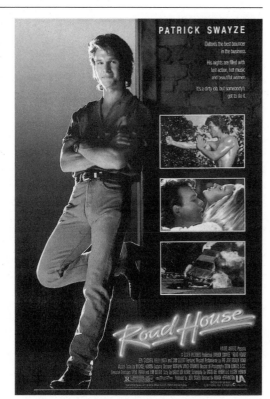

bones broken in a single film. Though each of these did middling box office business, Swayze was definitely on the wrong path here.

And then came 1990's *Ghost*, the biggest blockbuster any of its three stars (Swayze, Demi Moore, and Whoopi Goldberg) had ever made. Swayze had found a new niche, the romantic leading man, and played it to the hilt. Unfortunately, since then, he has made one wrong move after another. In 1991, he appeared in the action flick *Point Break*, which didn't live up to its box office potential. In 1992, *City of Joy* was released, featuring Swayze as a doctor finding himself by working with the street people of Calcutta, India. A quality film, *City of Joy* had no drawing power among Swayze's fans and therefore performed abominably at theaters. In 1993, Swayze's *Father Hood* was gone before most people realized it had even arrived.

The actor, and his fans, await another *Ghost* or *Dirty Dancing*, but at this point, even a *Road House* will do.

***

PART TWO: FILM DIRECTORS

The criteria for selection here are substantially similar to those of the previous section, with several obvious differences. While an actor may not get the lead role in a film for many years, a film has only one director. Though directors often make commercials, episodes of TV series, documentaries, short films, and school productions, I have limited myself to those whose first nationally released feature film was a hit followed by a bomb.

There were several directors who did not make the final cut here, including Ridley Scott and Clint Eastwood. Scott was excised because upon researching his second film (after the hit *Alien*), the quintessential sci-fi epic *Blade Runner*, it quickly became apparent that the film did not do as poorly in its original release as Hollywood myth has always claimed.

Eastwood was another story. His first directorial effort was the now-classic *Play Misty For Me*. His second, the ghostly western *High Plains Drifter*, did quite well in theaters. The director's third effort, *Breezy*, which was released the same year as *High Plains Drifter*, but which for some time I believed was released previous to it, is long forgotten and nearly classified as "lost." As such, it seems appropriate to at least mention the film here, though it does not qualify as a *sophomore* slump.

Breezy was the first film Eastwood directed in which he did not also star. In fact, he did not appear in it at all. The film was released by Universal in 1973 and starred William Holden and Kay Lenz. Not only have few people seen *Breezy*, but, like *Rebel*, with Sylvester Stallone, most have never even heard of the film. In fact, Eastwood's own assistant did not know much about it, except to say that "Clint has a copy of it in his own collection." As to the film's quality, who can say? It seems unlikely, however, that those of us who didn't see it in its original release will ever get the chance.

It's very possible that some of the following directors would like to make their "slump" films disappear as completely.

EMILE ARDOLINO

The late director must have felt as if he had gotten on a roller coaster when his first feature, *Dirty Dancing*, became a $63 million blockbuster. The film, already discussed elsewhere in these pages, was packed with music and dancing and, though thin in spots, is actually quite enjoyable. Interestingly enough,

Ardolino's is the third career that was basically "made" by *Dirty Dancing*.

Though star Patrick Swayze, a former dancer who stars as a dance instructor, had been in one minor success, this was his breakout film. His costar, Jennifer Grey, who played "Baby," also became a star based on the strength of *Dirty Dancing*, her chemistry with Swayze, and perhaps the dancing itself. The film also featured Cynthia Rhodes, who had previously appeared in only bombs. Curiously, after her one hit, Rhodes has appeared in virtually nothing.

Emile Ardolino's second film is a species all too common in Hollywood. *Chances Are* is a funny, heartwarming comedy with an excellent cast, a good script, and a great theme song, and yet, absolutely nobody went to see it. Playing with ideas already seen in such films as *Here Comes Mr. Jordan* and *Heaven Can Wait*, Robert Downey Jr. is a college student whose soul is reincarnated from the late husband of Cybill Shepherd. Improperly "processed" after his

After *Dirty Dancing* heated up ballrooms all over the world, Emile Ardolino directed a much better film, *Chances Are*, but it failed at the box office. © Copyright 1989 Tri-Star Pictures Inc. All rights reserved.

death, his soul's prior memory begins to return even as he finds himself about to become involved with "his" daughter (Mary Stuart Masterson).

Once his memory has returned, Downey's character must contend with Masterson's advances, revealing the truth to his former wife and trying to persuade her new beau, his former best friend (Ryan O'Neal), that he's on the level. All of the cast members are good, but Downey, as usual, is particularly engaging. With this film, Ardolino crafted a guilty pleasure, often found on cable and impossible to turn off. Critics were mildly entertained, though *Newsweek*'s David Ansen complained that "Ardolino's fantasy grows increasingly labored as it piles improbability upon psychological impossibility."

Unfortunately, as noted above, audiences ignored the film, shelling out a paltry $16 million to see it, and most people will probably never have heard of it. Ardolino went on to direct two other films, *Three Men and a Little Lady*, which was the sequel to *Three Men and a Baby*, and the Whoopi Goldberg blockbuster, *Sister Act*. All in all, a fairly good track record. Unfortunately, Ardolino died on November 20, 1993, at the age of fifty, from complications due to AIDS.

CLIVE BARKER

Clive Barker, whom Stephen King has called "the future of horror," first came to America's attention with the publication of three volumes of short stories, *The Books of Blood*. Barker followed with several more volumes of stories, and novels such as *The Damnation Game*, *Weaveworld*, *Imajica*, and *The Thief of Always*, which run the gamut from all-out horror to fantasy to children's fables. The author has created a number of popular comic book series and now is releasing computer games based on his work.

In 1986, in *Night Visions*, an anthology, Barker published a novella called *The Hellbound Heart*. A year later, the film version, directed by Barker himself, hit the screen under the title *Hellraiser*. A gruesome, chilling film, *Hellraiser* concerns the efforts of a man trying to escape from the "hell" where his actions have led him, and from the Cenobites, a race of demons who are charged with keeping him there. While Barker's direction is sometimes heavy-handed, the atmosphere of the film and its rich symbolism take it a step above most modern horror movies.

Audiences ate it up. *Hellraiser* was not a hit by then current Hollywood standards, but in a genre that had been experiencing rapidly decreasing box office success, its $11.5 million, and huge video rentals, were impressive indeed. Fans welcomed the bizarre cosmology of the film, and when it was done, clamored for more. In fact, three sequels have been made, with greater and lesser degrees of success, though all have done very well on video, and the main Cenobite character, "Pinhead," has become a pop culture icon. Barker chose not to direct the later installments of the series, however, taking instead a range of different producer credits.

The second film the author directed, *Nightbreed*, is another story entirely. Based on Barker's novella *Cabal*, the convoluted film has a man named Boone (Craig Sheffer) convinced by his psychiatrist that he is a serial killer, when it is the psychiatrist himself (played by director David Cronenberg) who is the murderer. Boone runs off to Canada in search of a place he has dreamed of, Midian, a city of monsters where he believes they will have to take him in because he too is a monster. Finding Midian, Boone is attacked and killed and does, actually, become a monster. His girlfriend, Lori, the police, the psychiatrist, and an insane priest all eventually track him down.

Nightbreed is a fascinating film, with the most extraordinary and exotic monsters ever put on screen. They are the good guys, and the rest, the "normals," are the villains. In a way, the film is a thinly veiled discussion of prejudice. While it loses its way at times, and the ending is a confusing mishmash that can be unraveled only by those who've read the novella, it is still quite enjoyable. The film prompted *The Boston Globe*'s Betsy Sherman to gush, "Clive Barker could be the savior of the horror movie . . . terrific horror fantasy."

Nightbreed was originally intended to be the first film in a series, as *Cabal* was intended to be the first story in a series. Unfortunately, the film fared poorly in theaters, finding a niche only upon its video release. The blame for *Nightbreed*'s failure is not the film's, but that of the company that released it, Morgan Creek.

The company basically dumped the film into theaters, having apparently already written it off as a failure. What little marketing it had was awful and completely off target. Though they could have chosen to showcase the monsters, and the interesting and original presentation of them in the film, Morgan Creek instead attempted to market *Nightbreed* like a bad seventies slasher film. Trailers and ads showed a woman being chased and a man with a knife. The original posters were boring and again promoted the idea that this was your basic mad-killer-on-the-loose film.

Looking at the numbers, it's hard to differentiate between *Hellraiser* and *Nightbreed*, which earned roughly $3 million less than the former film. In defining the success of the first and the failure of the latter, we must look at expectations and returns. Nobody expected *Hellraiser* to be the hit it was, but it was well executed and well marketed, and got attention from the press everywhere. *Nightbreed* was burdened with expectations high enough that they scared off its distributor, it was poorly marketed, and the press almost completely ignored it.

More successful was another Barker-based film, which he did not direct, *Candyman*. However, Barker is finally scheduled to direct another film, *Lord of Illusion* based upon Harry D'Amour, an occult detective he created, and who will be played by Scott Bakula, of TV's *Quantum Leap*.

PAUL BRICKMAN

"There's a time for playing it safe," the ad read, "and a time for *Risky Business*."

Risky Business was the story of Joel Goodsen (Tom Cruise), an upper-middle-class high school kid living in the suburbs of Chicago, who follows his raging hormones right into trouble. After calling for a prostitute (Rebecca De Mornay) named Lana to come to the house, a series of unlikely events leads to her becoming his temporary girlfriend and business partner as they turn his parents' home into a whorehouse for the weekend.

When the film debuted in 1983, it looked like just another crude coming-of-age sex comedy, along the lines of *Class* and *Private Lessons*. But that was the farthest thing from the truth. Instead, it was a warm, funny, stylish film that launched the careers of two stars, one of whom would become one of the biggest box office draws the world has ever known. With a kind of self-deprecating humor, *Risky Business* became one of those rare films that received what is known in the trades as "repeat business." Audiences were seeing the movie multiple times.

Like many successful films of the eighties, *Risky Business* was packed full of memorable dialogue. "Sometimes you've just gotta say what the fuck." "Porsche . . . there is no substitute." "I think he got on his bike, pedaled home, and whacked off." All of which you have to see the film to truly appreciate, right along with Cruise's underwear dance to Bob Seger's "Old Time Rock 'n' Roll."

Cruise had previously appeared in *The Outsiders* and *Taps*, and starred in a lame teen film called *Losin' It*, which was much closer to *Private Lessons* than to *Risky Business*. His smile, earnest charm, and comic timing made him an instant superstar. De Mornay was an unknown at the time, and though she did not take as much advantage of the successful spring-board the film provided, the sexy toughness she exhibited in *Risky Business* made her a star as well.

For first time director Paul Brickman, it had to have been a dream come true. *Newsweek* called *Risky Business* a "fresh, hypnotic and very sexy movie.... It's a dream version of a boy's sexual awakening, and like a dream it can tip unexpectedly from frolic to fever to nightmare." High praise indeed, and yet, strangely, after *Risky Business*, Brickman did not

Paul Brickman followed *Risky Business* with *Men Don't Leave*. Audiences didn't come. © Copyright 1990 Geffen Film Company. All rights reserved.

direct a feature film for seven years. Seven years! The only plausible explanation for this is that Brickman was familiar with the old Hollywood adage, "You're only as good as your latest film," and wanted to play it safe. Barring that, his absence after such success is inexplicable.

When his next work graced the screen, in 1990, Brickman fell under the same unfortunate circumstances that had cursed both Ardolino and Barker. He created a solid, enjoyable film, perhaps even an excellent film, and nobody went to see it.

Men Don't Leave is the story of a woman fighting to stay close to her sons after the tragic death of their father. In this heartwarming and, believe it or not, funny film, Jessica Lange is the mother, Chris O'Donnell her eldest son, and the always wonderful Joan Cusack is his much older girlfriend. Arliss Howard also stars as the new man in Lange's life. It's hard to imagine a better cast and, in fact, it's even more difficult to understand why this film was not at least a modest success at the box office. It made just over $6 million. Alas, such are the whims of the mercurial moviegoing public.

Lange and Cusack are polar opposites, and though *Men Don't Leave* was the first film to bring the talented newcomer Chris O'Donnell into the spotlight, it is really the interaction between the two actresses that comprises the best parts of the film. The struggle is between Cusack, who acts with this younger man, as if she's just brought home a wonderful pet, and Lange, who has already lost one man in her life and will be damned if she allows another one to go, at least before she's ready.

Despite hailing the film's "seductive style, uniformly fine acting and glimmers of real substance," *Newsweek*'s David Ansen called *Men Don't Leave* "a frustrating failure." Though he decried what he considered implicit sexism in the film, he did not really make a case for such a drastic statement.

Whatever. Rent it and decide for yourself.

Let's just hope we don't have to wait another seven years for Brickman's next project.

AMY HECKERLING

In the late seventies, writer Cameron Crowe returned to his high school and wrote a book about his days there, which was made into the 1982 film, *Fast Times at Ridgemont High*. Despite a trashing in *Time*, which asserted that "director Amy Heckerling has failed to provide the raunch or poignancy that would interest young moviegoers," the film was a milestone for America's teens, earning $32 million at the box office. As sophomoric as some of the comedy is, there are also many genuinely funny moments, and some painful memories of growing up are bound to be recalled in any viewing of the film.

The stellar young cast of *Fast Times* included Jennifer Jason Leigh, Judge Reinhold, Phoebe Cates, and, of course, Sean Penn as the inimitable Jeff Spicoli. In a year that also brought us *Porky's*, a film of far more base and prurient intent and with far less real amusement (though it made more money), *Fast Times* seemed nearly brilliant in comparison. In any case, some of the best moments of the year were Penn's. The actor portrayed Spicoli as the coolest, and absolutely the stupidest, kid in school. It would probably not be much of an extrapolation to see the influence of Spicoli in everything from *Teenage Mutant Ninja Turtles* ("Over here, pizza dude!") to *Beavis & Butthead*.

Director Amy Heckerling knows her audience intimately. Reinhold's Brad is much too serious about his fast-food employment, and an obsessive masturbatory fantasy about his little sister's best friend (Cates), who interrupts him in the act, so to speak. His sister, played by Leigh, has her share of serious problems. And all the while, Spicoli spices up the film with inane comments and out and out stupidity. Look for Anthony Edwards and Eric Stoltz as Penn's "Buds" in the film.

Heckerling's second directorial effort was vastly different from the first. With much broader comedy and packed with the goofiest of one-liners, *Johnny Dangerously* was a no-brainer. Relying heavily on the comic timing of star Michael Keaton, the film does have its share of laughs. Overall, however, the film is as dumb as Heckerling's debut film was smart.

Keaton plays an up-and-coming young mobster named, you guessed it, Johnny Dangerously. He falls for moll Marilu Henner and faces off against another "mug" who turned on him, Joe Piscopo. Much of the film is gag humor, which works wonders in a three-minute sketch on *Saturday Night Live* but is hard to sustain in a ninety-minute movie. And Heckerling doesn't sustain it. Keaton had already carved himself out a fan following through his fabulously funny performance in *Night Shift*, and this ought to have been that good. Unfortunately it wasn't, and the box office numbers reflected this. While it had a long life on home video, *Johnny Dangerously* earned only half what Heckerling's freshman effort had, despite Keaton's considerable popularity.

Strangely, Heckerling's third film was even worse. *National Lampoon's European Vacation* was a sequel to the hit Chevy Chase comedy, and Chase returned as Clark Griswold. While the third in the series, *National Lampoon's Christmas Vacation*, is quite funny, Heckerling's middle installment is boring and in some places downright stupid, with only small

Amy Heckerling followed *Fast Times at Ridgemont High* with *Johnny Dangerously* and probably wishes she hadn't. Copyright © 1984 Twentieth Century Fox Film Corp. All rights reserved.

flashes of the humor that made the original so entertaining. ("Look kids, Big Ben!") The charm of the original is gone, and the actors playing the Griswold children are horrendous.

From there, however, Heckerling went on to enjoy the biggest success of her career. Not to mention that *Look Who's Talking* was the major comeback film for John Travolta (whether Heckerling did us a favor, we may never know). The film's gimmick, allowing audiences to hear the thoughts of Kirstie Alley's new baby (in Bruce Willis's voice no less), works tremendously well, and the leads give you that warm feeling inside as they romance one another. Without the gimmick, it might not have made the money it did. Who can say?

The first sequel, unimaginatively titled *Look Who's Talking Too*, was the original's polar opposite. Unfunny to a fault, it seems as if every joke fails. The audience is left with the same discomfort one feels when watching a comedian really die on stage. This one has the voices of Roseanne Arnold and Damon Wayans as well as Willis's, but even that doesn't do the trick. Whatever Heckerling did right with *Look Who's Talking*, she must have decided to reverse when she went to make the sequel.

DENNIS HOPPER

Unfortunately, *Easy Rider* loses something in the translation between the late sixties and the mid-nineties. Made on a shoestring budget, the film was a major success in its American release in 1969, already having been named Best Film by a New Director at the Cannes Film Festival for that year. Still, it's an odd little film.

Odd enough, in fact, that *Newsweek*'s Joe Morgenstein ran a full page review that read as if it had been written by two people. The initial three quarters of the piece trashes the movie.

"Time and again," Morgenstein wrote, "I wanted to reach out and shake Peter Fonda and Dennis Hopper ... until they stopped their damned-fool pompous poeticizing."

He goes on to say many unflattering things about the film and its performances, and yet, in the final quarter of the review, he praises it as "an important movie that's sure to involve a large audience in its story

Dennis Hopper's *Easy Rider* celebrated guys getting stoned, but *The Last Movie* just sank like one. *Copyright © Universal Pictures.*

of two foolish, decent hippies set upon by indecent squares. . . . [It's] not consistently well made, but it is purposefully made. And the purpose pays off."

In the duality of that review lies the problem in watching *Easy Rider* today. Though in retrospect we can understand why Morgenstein makes his latter comments, time has made it almost impossible for us to agree with him. On the other hand, the majority of his comments about the film's silly aspects are still valid today.

The story of Wyatt ("Captain America") and Billy, played by Peter Fonda and director Dennis Hopper, respectively, the film takes its protagonists from a lucrative drug deal, cross country via Harley Davidson, and through a meandering series of events that are intended to teach them, and the audience, that anyone attempting to be "free" in America, to operate outside the system our society has set up, will be oppressed, vilified, and eventually killed for their freedom. Pretty depressing.

Along the way, the audience is treated to Jack Nicholson's great, small, Oscar-nominated performance as an alcoholic lawyer who represents America's forced sense of false propriety, the chains that bind individuals, according to the themes of the film. The moment he attempts freedom, Nicholson's character is instantly, and fatally, punished.

Seen in this light, *Easy Rider* could be talking just as easily about America as we near the turn of the century. However, because it is couched in the cinematic language of the sixties, with hippie communes and acid trips and people who say "dig it," many viewers will find it hard to glean such inferences from the film. On the other hand, the glory of the American landscape is still vividly portrayed in the film, its ending is still violent poetry, and Nicholson's performance will always be entrancing.

Having already appeared in films as diverse as *Rebel Without a Cause* and *The Trip*, Hopper was just trying his hand at directing, and working from a script he cowrote with Peter Fonda and Terry Southern. The film made $42.5 million at the box office—in 1969! Though Hopper went on to success as an actor (and little as a director), Fonda continued to try his hand at both acting and directing, with minimal success.

Actors who become directors are always subject to more scrutiny than directors who start out that way. For some, like Eastwood, Redford, Beatty, and Costner (so far), it turns out very well. For others, however, who might make a mistake or two, the vultures are always there, waiting to pounce. *Easy Rider* had made Hopper a hot commodity. The spotlight was on full-blast when his second directorial effort hit screens in 1971. It may as well have been a searchlight, trying to determine where this movie was going and where it disappeared to.

You've got to wonder what Hopper was thinking when he made *The Last Movie*. The story revolves around relationships among the members of a film production crew, beginning as they wrap shooting in a small village in Peru, of all places. *The Last Movie* begins nowhere and goes, essentially, nowhere that is decipherable. Even though the director had just come off a hit, you've got to wonder why the cast, which included Kris Kristofferson, Sylvia Miles, Dean Stockwell, and, of course, Fonda again, would ever have signed on to this film after reading the script.

What were they thinking? Unsurprisingly, this is another of those few films that Exhibitor Relations has no box office records for. Makes you wonder if there was any box office at all, doesn't it?

The Last Movie had a fascinating effect on Hopper's directorial career, stopping it dead in its tracks for more than a decade. In 1983, he directed himself in the gritty but forgotten film, *Out of the Blue*. Then, in 1988, he returned to the helm with the controversial and mildly successful Robert Duvall and Sean Penn cops vs. gangs film, *Colors*. A powerful film, and the total antithesis of Hopper's previous efforts, *Colors* nevertheless has inexplicably disappeared, like so many films of recent years, from pop culture's RAM. Less successful, though just as easily forgotten, were Hopper's two 1990 efforts, *The Hot Spot* and the cable original *Backtrack*, with Jodie Foster.

These days, if Hopper is remembered as a director at all, it is generally for his first film, *Easy Rider*. Though he made the talk show rounds promoting his 1994 Tom Berenger and Erika Eleniak turkey, *Chasers*, the film opened in sixteenth place, earning less than three quarters of a million dollars.

MICHAEL LEHMANN

"*Heathers* was that rare exception," Veronica Chambers wrote in the April 1994 issue of *Premiere*, "a movie with influence far beyond its $1 million box office."

This is a dicey one, isn't it? How can a film that grossed only a measly million dollars at the box office be a hit? Well, that would depend on its intentions. In earlier portions of this book, certain art house films that were never intended to make money were trashed. While some of these films are technically included because of their low ticket sales (which may well have been expected by the producers and distributors), they were actually included because they were, more or less, *bad* movies.

That said, *Heathers* was indeed a success on several levels. First, it started a lot of people talking about a little black comedy by a first-time director with unknown actors. Second, it turned a profit. Third, it was a big hit on video. And finally, it launched major careers for Michael Lehmann and his two stars, Christian Slater and Winona Ryder.

Ryder is Veronica, a girl quickly growing sick of hanging out with the vicious, "cool" clique at school, all of whom are named Heather except for her. Slater is J.D., the new kid, who scores with a Jack Nicholson–influenced attitude, making enemies fast. When the two hook up, J.D. starts to show his stripes as a true lunatic, and the young lovers start offing the cool kids. Perhaps the most appropriate moment is when they make two macho jocks appear to have killed each other in a homosexual suicide pact. Funny, creepy, at times chilling, *Heathers* is a masterwork.

As a team, the lead pair is magical, and Lehmann makes extraordinary use of their chemistry. The script is another triumph. When the aforementioned jocks tell J.D. that his new high school doesn't accept gays, meaning him, Slater leans back in his chair, boots on the table, and cracks, "They seem to have an open door policy on assholes, though." Ah, it's a victory for all those kids who wish they'd had the intestinal fortitude to use such a line against jerks like these two!

Newsweek's David Ansen practically gushed.

"As black as pitch," he wrote, "this twisted comedy of high school horrors is a work of genuine audacity. . . . When *Heathers* hits its stride, it reaches wild and original comic highs."

Slater went on to *Pump Up the Volume*, *Robin Hood*, *True Romance*, *Untamed Heart*, and *Interview With a Vampire*. Ryder went on to *Edward Scissorhands*, *Dracula*, *Age of Innocence*, and *The House of Spirits*. Lehmann, on the other hand, went on to *Meet the Applegates*.

Wha? Meet the who?

Exactly.

The year after *Heathers*, *Meet the Applegates* played in very limited release and then took the short road to video oblivion. Nobody saw it. At all. (Okay, maybe one or two, but nobody who'll admit it—it made less than half a million dollars.) Ed Begley Jr. and Stockard Channing (a recent Oscar nomination shows how far one can come in four years) star in this abysmal film about a family of huge cockroaches living a double life, masquerading as human beings even as they plan the nuclear destruction of humanity.

Intelligent art house managers will start showing this as a double feature with David Cronenberg's *Naked Lunch* (if you don't get the reference, rent them both and do it yourself).

"Lehmann really messes up," wrote *Rolling Stone*'s Peter Travers. "The picture sinks, but Lehmann doesn't—he has enough talent percolating just below the surface of this film to make us eager for his next."

Yeah, well, sorry to disappoint you, Peter.

Based on the success of *Heathers*, Lehmann was hired to helm the next big project from mega-star Bruce Willis. It was going to be a huge success, with an all-star

109

After *Heathers*, one of the most auspicious directorial debuts of the 1980s, Michael Lehmann made *Meet the Applegates*, a film about cockroaches. Then he made *Hudson Hawk*. Copyright © 1989 New World Entertainment. All rights reserved.

cast including Danny Aiello, Sandra Bernhard, Andie MacDowell, and James Coburn. It was going to be . . . but it wasn't. Instead, the pantheon of the most colossal movie failures of all time—*Heaven's Gate, Howard the Duck, Ishtar*—now added Michael Lehmann's *Hudson Hawk* to its ranks. While the film made far more than either of Lehmann's earlier films, in comparison to its skyrocketing budget, it was an incredible turkey.

Oh, for the days of small budgets, small risks, and great rewards!

Lehmann's fourth film, *Airheads*, starred Brendan Fraser, Steve Buscenci, and Adam Sandler as a struggling rock band who take over a radio station and force the DJ to play their songs. An amusing concept, executed with nothing resembling the style and dark grit of *Heathers*. The film did mediocre box office, and went away.

GEORGE A. ROMERO

For the greatest amusement, I feel forced to reprint Vincent Canby's *New York Times* review of *Night of the Living Dead* in its entirety.

"*Night of the Living Dead*," Canby wrote, "is a grainy little movie acted by what appear to be nonprofessional actors, who are besieged in a farm house by some other nonprofessional actors who stagger around, stiff-legged, pretending to be flesh-eating ghouls.

"The dialogue and background music sound hollow, as if they had been recorded in an empty swimming pool, and the wobbly camera seems to have a fetishist's interest in hands, clutched, wrung, scratched, severed and finally—in the ultimate assumption—eaten like pizza.

"The movie, which was made by some people in Pittsburgh, opened yesterday at the New Amsterdam Theater on 42nd Street and at other theaters around town."

"Some people in Pittsburgh." Romero must have loved that one. Canby's 108-word review of *Night of the Living Dead* is one long disparaging remark, and he couldn't have been farther off the mark. the importance of Romero's *Night of the Living Dead* to the evolution of the horror film has been greatly examined and cannot possibly be overstated.

Conversely, the film's influence on mainstream filmmaking is often ignored completely. Unlike previous horror and science-fiction films, *Night of the Living Dead* offers no scientific explanation for its plot (the dead rise and begin chomping on the living . . . duh!) or any romantic subplots. In a broader sense, two of the most important developments in the film were the race of the lead character and the ground-breaking ending.

First, the film's star, Duane Jones, was black, a fact that is largely overlooked in hindsight, even though such casting was still uncommon at the time (except for "blaxploitation" flicks, and stories in which the role demanded a person of color). In truth, the white characters in John A. Russo's script are offered up in two flavors, moronic or just plain dumb. Jones's character seems to be the only intelligent human left alive.

111

Second, after a valiant effort to fend off the zombies until help arrives, all of the people in the house are eventually killed except Jones. The ending shows Jones waking on a sunny morning, walking out onto the porch even as help finally appears, only to be shot in the head by red-necks who think he's a zombie. Now that's an ending.

The ultimate low-budget cheapie, made for almost nothing, the film earned more than $6.5 million, many times what it cost to make.

Night of the Living Dead, which had been greatly influenced by Richard Matheson's wonderful novel *I Am Legend* and the film starring Vincent Price adapted from it, *The Last Man on Earth*, in turn produced an extraordinary number of sequels and imitations. In fact, the movie has become a genre unto itself. Romero did two sequels, the blackly comedic classic *Dawn of the Dead* and the disappointing *Day of the Dead*, and produced a remake of the original in 1990. Italian directors like Lucio Fulci have ripped Romero off quite consistently, and several comedies have been made using the premise, including a trilogy of *Return of the Living Dead* films, and the entertaining and vastly underrated *Night of the Comet*.

Romero's second film is an obscure and long-forgotten relationship comedy called *It's Always Vanilla*. The film is apparently so bad that the director has been said to pretend it does not exist.

Romero has gone on to direct such frightening fare as Stephen King's *Creepshow* and *The Dark Half*, *Monkey Shines*, and cult favorites such as

Martin and *The Crazies*. It is hard to imagine, with such inventive fare on his resumé, that Romero could have crafted such a boring tale of horror as *Season of the Witch* (aka *Hungry Wives*, *Jack's Wife*), his third film which was released in 1972. The film revolves around a young suburban housewife who fills the emptiness in her life by murdering her husband and joining a coven of witches. Trust me, it only *sounds* like a good movie.

In the wake of the success of his first film, *Season of the Witch* was a commercial disaster, yet another film not in the records of Exhibitor Relations. Unlike some other Romero films that fared poorly at the box office, this film deserved that fate. A rerelease in 1982, attempting to capitalize on the success of *Dawn of the Dead*, fared no better than the first effort.

The only saving grace of the film, which seems to carry a perverse feminist message, is the comic touch Romero adds to certain scenes, as if to let the audience know that he's not taking the whole thing too seriously. Unfortunately, such humor is subtle and there is not nearly enough of it to make the film an actual black comedy, which would clearly have been a more fruitful creative avenue for the director, but probably would not have altered its box office fate in any way.

Originally released as *Jack's Wife* and then altered to *Hungry Wives*, the title was changed to *Season of the Witch* upon its 1982 rerelease. A curious choice, as an equally bad film, *Halloween III: Season of the Witch*, which had nothing to do with the rest of that series, was playing in theaters at the time.

113

RON SHELTON

Kevin Costner had already become a star thanks to his performances in such hits as *No Way Out* and *The Untouchables*. But really, it was *Bull Durham* that put him over the top. When Crash Davis, Costner's character, gives Annie Savoy (Susan Sarandon) that memorable speech about "long, slow, deep, wet kisses that last for three days," women all over America were convinced that here was a leading man to live up to the Cary Grants and Clark Gables of yesteryear. Sarandon was also already a star, though her biggest hit, *Thelma & Louise* was still in the future. Even Tim Robbins, who is billed as a newcomer and whose performance is hysterical, had made a couple of movies before *Bull Durham* (one of which, likely to his regret, was *Howard the Duck*).

It seems highly unlikely that a studio would hire a director who had never directed a feature film before to helm *Bull Durham*. And yet, that's precisely what they did. Ron Shelton, who also wrote the screenplay, delivered one of the most thoroughly enjoyable films of 1988, drawing incredible performances out of his entire cast and forcing his audience to wonder if there had ever been a baseball film made before this one. Certainly, baseball had never been this much fun.

Bull Durham was the story of a former major league pitcher brought onto a minor league team to cultivate a wild rookie pitcher, who then falls for the local baseball groupie who hooks up with a different player every year. The eccentricities of Sarandon's Annie, the blatant stupidity of Robbins's "Nuke" LaLoosh and the heated charm of Costner's Crash are priceless roles in a film that will have a very long life. Even without the compulsory comparison to some of Costner's later, lesser romantic efforts, such as the absurd *Revenge* and the insulting, banal *The Bodyguard*, the film is a gem.

And it earned more than $50 million. Suddenly, Ron Shelton was very hot.

Setting up his second film, a drama this time, the hot young director would have been justified in expecting another hit. It had a lot going for it. A true story, detailing the fiery,

Ron Shelton became a hot young director after *Bull Durham*. The cool reception to *Blaze*, starring Lolita Davidovich and Paul Newman, was unexpected. Copyright © Touchstone Pictures. All rights reserved. Photo Credit: Sidney Baldwin.

controversial relationship between 1950s Louisiana governor Earl K. Long and the famous French Quarter stripper, Blaze Starr. A voluptuous, talented newcomer named Lolita Davidovitch. Strippers. Paul Newman, the ultimate leading man.

How could it miss?

Shelton probably asked himself that very same question when the film didn't make it to the $20 million mark. Though the film had a respectable video and cable afterlife, and despite the fact that it had all those elements in its favor, and that it is, after all is said and done, an interesting little film, it petered out because it is also incredibly boring.

Boring? A film about political corruption, New Orleans, and naked women boring?

Well, um, yeah.

Time's Richard Corliss wrote that "Shelton directs *Blaze* with plenty of pungent wit, but from a high disinterested view. He never gets steam into the affair."

Shelton's next film showed where he went wrong. the writer-director ought to have stuck with the winning combination of *Bull Durham*, sports, comedy, and sex. *White Men Can't Jump* starred Wesley Snipes, Woody Harrelson, and Rosie Perez in a tale of basketball hustling in L.A. It was Shelton's script and direction that eased Harrelson's transition from TV star to movie star. Snipes's fast talking and the pair's mutually insulting tirades, as well as

Perez's star turn as a *Jeopardy*-obsessed "former disco queen from Brooklyn, New York" made it an instant hit. Talk of a sequel still rages.

Shelton continued the sports theme into his latest film, *Blue Chips*, about corruption in college basketball, but he left out the most important element . . . the laughs. A straight drama starring Nick Nolte and Shaquille O'Neal, the film did passably well, but didn't pull in the business of *White Men Can't Jump*.

JOHN SINGLETON

In the wake of a sea of similarly themed films, some hack jobs and some of real quality, it is harder for *Boyz 'n the Hood* to stand out, but stand out it does. The writer-director was 23-year-old Singleton, and *Boyz* was his first effort.

Newsweek's Ansen wrote that the film "is the work of a truly gifted film-maker. . . . There are subtler, more polite movies around, but none made out of such a heart-stopping sense of urgency. . . . Singleton's powerhouse movie has the impact of a stun gun."

Wow. No wonder it made more than $56 million and was an enormous video hit.

Riding the wave of a new era of black filmmaking, with a respect and box office clout that was relatively new (and thanks, in large part, to Spike Lee), black directors were able to rise above the blaxploitation films of two decades earlier. But none quite as well as Singleton.

Boyz 'n the Hood starts as a tale of gang violence, but at its most fundamental, its elements are those of a much more classic tragedy. Cuba Gooding Jr. and Ice Cube play young men growing up in the 'hood, the crossfire of rapidly deteriorating South Central Los Angeles. Friends from childhood, Gooding is on the college track thanks to a father (Laurence Fishburne) who pushes him, and Ice Cube is being pushed away from his family, toward the gangs. Though the tale is ostensibly Gooding's, it is Ice Cube's life that is most telling. His older brother is the smart one, the talented one, the "good" one, and so his own family has cast him in the role of the "bad" son. He never had a chance.

Two men, coming of age in the same surroundings but in vastly different circumstances, trying to escape the terrors and the grief of their world and finding it next to impossible. That is the story of *Boyz 'n the Hood*, and it is a timeless one. A classic drama, the film deserved all of the attention it received and earned every ticket sale that led to its success.

Singleton was hailed as a wunderkind. He drew raves across the board and was so hot that rumors flew about his attachment to numerous Hollywood projects. In fact, he was even said to be preparing to direct the screen version of Marvel Comics' superhero, *The Black Panther*. What Singleton was really doing, though, was working on the screenplay for his next film, which he would also direct, *Poetic Justice*.

Poetic Justice seemed like a natural. Superstar Janet Jackson was signed

118

to star as a young urban poet, a year after Whitney Houston had starred in *The Bodyguard*. The poetry was written by Maya Angelou, perhaps the most famous living practitioner of that art. Actor-rapper Tupac Shakur also starred in this film about the coming of age of Jackson's character, sort of a "Girlz 'n the Hood." How could it miss?

How, indeed?

While *Poetic Justice* was not a complete box office failure, earning $27.5 million, it fell far short of the expectations set up for it by Singleton's cheering section and the box office performance of *Boyz 'n the Hood*. And the critics, who had universally hailed his first film, were just as unanimous in their drubbing of his second. In truth, periodicals as well respected as *Time* and the *Wall Street Journal*, as well as such critics as Joel Siegel, actually recommended that audiences stay away from the film, so low was their opinion of it.

119

After John Singleton received a rookie year best director nomination for *Boyz 'n the Hood*, Hollywood thought he could do no wrong. Then he made *Poetic Justice*, with Janet Jackson and Tupac Shakur. *Copyright © 1993 Columbia Pictures.*

The title of Anthony Lane's *New Yorker* review alone was a major jab at the film—"Blank Verse." After trashing it, he ends with the line, "I think her [Justice's] parents should have called her License."

Still, despite the failure of *Poetic Justice*, Singleton has enough power based upon his first film to keep working on his own projects for years to come. Next up for the writer-director is *Higher Learning*, which he will also produce. The film will team Singleton once again with Laurence Fishburne and Ice Cube, actors who had a large part in making *Boyz 'n the Hood* as real as it was, and as much of a hit as it turned out to be. Perhaps that reunion will put Singleton back on track.

STEVEN SODERBERGH

A funny, uncomfortable, and quirky little film, Soderbergh's debut directorial effort, *sex, lies & videotape*, won the Palme d'Or at the Cannes Film Festival in 1989, the equivalent of the Best Picture Oscar. While such accolades were not forthcoming in America, the film did garner rave reviews from U.S. critics and had a respectable box office take. It also launched the film careers of two of its stars, Laura San Giacomo and Peter Gallagher, and boosted those of the other two, Andie MacDowell and James Spader.

"Steven Soderbergh . . . has the gift," David Ansen wrote. ". . . You're in the hands of a filmmaker who knows precisely what he's doing and you hang on every word."

Spader is a strange, insecure nerdy type who somehow manages to get women to reveal their innermost secrets, feelings, and urges to him during videotaped interviews and then gets off on watching them. When he visits an old college buddy, played by Gallagher, his videotape fetish is turned on Gallagher's wife (MacDowell) and her sister (San Giacomo). His probing and prodding leads to the revelation that Gallagher and San Giacomo have had an affair, a family tragedy seen through the lens of Spader's camera.

Kafka. Most people thought Steven Soderbergh's sophomore effort was just a nightmare. *Copyright © 1991 Miramax.*

The film is at times funny, touching, odd, disturbing, and sexy. The performances are uniformly excellent. Yet, while *sex, lies & videotape* was critically acclaimed, talked about all across the country, and did respectable business in theaters and on videotape, one film does not a career make. Soderbergh, like Singleton, is a writer-director, apparently interested only in filming his own work, and this has limited and perhaps even hurt him.

Something one must wonder about all such hot young filmmakers is, have the accolades, their early success, and the respect of their peers come too soon, too quickly, and, therefore, gone to their heads? Did that happen to Singleton? Did it happen to Soderbergh? After becoming the Next Big Thing, did the writer-director begin to believe his own press, as they say? There are two possible ways to explain Soderbergh's next project: Either he did believe his own press, and thought that anything he did would be embraced by critics and audiences alike; or he just didn't care, and wanted to make what he wanted to make, whether people liked it or not.

It is preferable, though more difficult, to believe the latter. In any case, Soderbergh's next project was a truly bizarre, misguided art film called *Kafka*. Shake off the director's pretensions, which include the black-and-white film used for the first two-thirds of the movie, and somewhere underneath it all there might have been a commercially viable thriller. As it was, however, almost nobody has even heard of the film, much less seen it. While *Sex, lies & videotape* pulled in $25 million at the box office, *Kafka* made less than a million.

Kafka is a fantasy riff on the life of Franz Kafka, played straight, "a surprisingly tepid and stiff pastiche," according to *Newsweek*. The film stars

Jeremy Irons (what was he thinking?) as the title character, an insurance company employee in early-twentieth-century Prague. Drawn into a web of intrigue as incomprehensible to the viewer as it is to Irons's character, he becomes completely paranoid, jumping at shadows. Also starring Theresa Russell, Alec Guiness, Joel Grey, and Ian Holm, *Kafka* is more of an aggravation than an entertainment.

Soderbergh's third film fared little better financially, but its packaging alone will make *King of the Hill* a depression-era tale of family conflict, a more viable video rental to many people.

Unlike many of the other directors who have experienced a sophomore slump, Soderbergh has yet to recover from his. Whether this is due to his creative choices or the lack of audience interest, or both, remains to be seen. In any case, it seems unlikely that Steven Soderbergh will ever produce anything as commercial as the current work of any of the other directors in this section.

PART THREE: MUSICAL ACTS

Unlike actors, most of whom struggle through years of small roles to get their first starring vehicle, and though some musicians start as studio players or members of a backup band, it is far more common for pop superstars to be born "overnight," with the release of their first work. This is because their first record is something all their own. The name on it is theirs, and so the accolades, or blame, belong to them and nobody else.

There are scores of musical acts that have hit it big with their first album or single . . . and so for the purposes of this book, hitting it big just wasn't good enough. No, here, the first album or single by a musical act must have hit number one in the pages of *Billboard* magazine to be included.

Most of the time, it takes years for an artist to climb to the top of the charts, and once there, stardom is difficult to sustain. However, it is not unheard of for an artist to hit the big time, number one on *Billboard*'s Hot 100, on his or her first time out of the box. Mariah Carey, for instance, had seven number one singles in a row.

On the other hand, many artists have hit the top spot with their first single ... and then never break into the top fifty again. Some never even hit the chart again. But for the most part, the criteria used here attempt to avoid one-hit-wonders, unless they have some other reason for sustained celebrity. Most fascinating, and therefore the majority of the material in this section, are those acts that have started at number one, suffered drastic drops with later releases, and later rebounded with hits placing at or near the top. Nearly all of these entries, out of both preference and necessity, revolve around songs rather than albums. Though it would have been simple to include every musical act to have suffered the required slump, those considered just plain boring have been left out. For the most part, a slump in this case was considered a fall from number one to forty or below, though there are several exceptions. All musical acts were chosen based upon their performance on *Billboard* magazine's American pop charts, which reflect national sales and airplay of music. However, in most cases, those releases indicated as the first efforts of the act in question are the actual first efforts, not taking into consideration that many performers recorded music for limited and local release before getting a major record deal.

All *Billboard* chart information quoted in this section is copyrighted by BPI Communications, Inc., and is used with their gracious permission.

So, hey, crank up your old beat-up stereo, put on your 8-tracks of Blue Swede and the Starland Vocal Band, and let's get rockin'.

THE ANIMALS

"There is a house in New Orleans . . ."

So sang Eric Burdon, vocalist for The Animals, on their eponymous 1964 debut album on the MGM record label. The song, "House of the Rising Sun," debuted on *Billboard*'s Hot 100 chart in August of that year and quickly rose to number one where it stayed for three weeks.

The Animals were a British rock act, part of the "Invasion" that had already begun and that left dozens of new groups jostling for position on the charts. They had begun their career in the clubs of Newcastle, England in the late 1950s, billing themselves as the Alan Price combo, after the group's keyboard player. In fact, from the time of their debut in America, it was singer Burdon, rather than Price, who garnered the attention.

The tale of a Louisiana whorehouse, "House of the Rising Sun" remains one of the best-known songs by The Animals, and interestingly enough, would end up being their only number one single. Though the band had great success with the first single from *The Animals* album, the second performed so poorly that it was nearly an embarrassment.

A bluesy tune called "Gonna Send You Back to Walker (Gonna Send You

Back to Georgia)," an unlikely release from a British band, hit radio the month after "House of the Rising Sun," spent only three weeks on the chart, and topped out at number fifty-seven, far below even being considered a "top forty" single, vital at that time. For the rest of their career, The Animals produced only two other singles that did not rise at least into the top half of the Hot 100. Part of the reason for the song's failure can be seen by examining the formula that resulted in the band's other hits.

Over the next two years, The Animals continued to churn out such legendary angry youth rock anthems as "Don't Let Me Be Misunderstood," "We Gotta Get Out of This Place" and "It's My Life." Just a sample of lyrics from each song's refrain would give a unique perspective into the thought processes of The Animals target audience, the youth of America, in 1965 when all three songs were on the charts:

It was a volatile year. In March, Martin Luther King Jr. led his "March of Freedom" from Selma to Montgomery, Alabama. For four days in the heat of August, riots raged on the streets of Watts in Los Angeles, and more than twelve thousand National Guardsmen were called in. At the beginning of the year, Vietnam had been almost a non-issue. By its end, nearly a quarter million American soldiers were already fighting there.

The next year, the group ostensibly broke up, with Burdon taking a new version, Eric Burdon & The Animals, through two more albums and a handful of hits. Bassist Bryan "Chas" Chandler went on to discover and then manage rock legend Jimi Hendrix, bringing him first back home to England where he became very hot.

The Animals broke up, seemingly for good, in 1968, only to come together once again in 1983, on I.R.S. Records. They toured the country with another sixties revival group, John Kay & Steppenwolf. Though their hits still resonated, they could not have the emotional impact on eighties teens that they had at the height of the most tumultuous time in twentieth-century America.

In a weird, almost arrogant turn, Burdon played the lead role in the 1982 film *Comeback*, about a blues-influenced rock singer trying to make it back to the top of the charts. Not much of a stretch, was it? On another film note, 1987 brought audiences a film called *House of the Rising Sun* an obvious swipe from The Animals, though the film and the song have nothing in common but the title. The film, in fact, is about as limp a murder mystery as you'll find, with nobody involved that you would ever have heard of.

PAUL ANKA

Generation X'ers will remember Anka for many of his later feats, especially his 1974 number one single, "(You're) Havin' My Baby," which spent three weeks at the top spot. Another of his big hits, "Put Your Head on My Shoulder," may be better remembered as a song crooned by Anson Williams as Potsie on *Happy Days*. Of course, the Anka song that is perhaps most ingrained in the brains of

America not only did not have vocals by the singer-songwriter, it didn't even have any words. The theme from *The Tonight Show Starring Johnny Carson* may have disappeared from the tube, but just about anyone over age eighteen can hum it if you ask.

All of this is only a slice of Anka's extraordinary career. Between 1957, when he scored his first number one on the eve of his sixteenth birthday, and 1983, when he still made it into the top forty with "Hold Me 'Til the Mornin' Comes," Anka had more than fifty singles hit *Billboard*'s Hot 100 chart, a dozen of which made it into the top ten. That incredible run was founded upon enthusiasm and support from his father, something many pop superstars are not fortunate enough to receive. Anka had performed since the age of twelve, and his father was generous enough to pay for the recording of his first single, a song that never hit the charts.

His first charted single was "Diana," and number one was a pretty extraordinary feat for a boy his age. It still is today. What is perhaps most fascinating about Anka's early days is not, incredibly, that "Diana" was a number one single, but that, after having that song spend twenty-nine weeks on the charts, racking up publicity and exposure enough to make him a star, it was still possible for his second single, "I Love You, Baby," to fall an extraordinary, heartbreaking ninety-six positions on the chart, to number ninety-seven.

While Anka went on to record such hits as "Lonely Boy," "Times of Your Life," and, of course, "Puppy Love," he was also an incredibly prolific songwriter whose work was recorded by everyone from Frank Sinatra to Tom Jones, including the timeless classic, "My Way."

But Anka's appeal went beyond that, stretching out to include television and film. In 1959 he appeared in the film *Girls Town*, starring Mamie Van Doren and featuring appearances by Mel Torme and the Platters, among others. Thirty-three years later he showed up on screen again in *Captain Ron*, a bomb starring Kurt Russell and Martin Short. In between, however, Anka was a common musical guest on many variety programs, hosting several, including *Hullabaloo* and *The Midnight Special*, and even appearing as himself on the short-lived 1960 police drama *Dan Raven*.

Paul Anka remains quite popular today and has been a fixture of Las Vegas casino entertainment for many years. Other than his prodigious songwriting abilities and his vocal talents, one reason for Anka's continued popularity could be that his music reminds audiences of a simpler time, a time when dates and dancing, holding hands, and broken hearts were all that really mattered in the world. Or perhaps it is only that, with Anka's help, that is how people can remember those times. In any case, with the recent resurgence in popularity of Frank Sinatra, Tony Ben-

After a number one debut, Paul Anka's second single "I Love You, Baby" stalled at number ninety-seven.

nett, and Nat "King" Cole (via daughter Natalie), it seems quite plausible that Anka will one day return to the Hot 100 chart. One thing is certain: He spent so long there that if he does return, he'll find his place all prepared, a groove worn smooth by his years on top.

TONI BASIL

Though I have and will continue to try to avoid one-hit-wonders, Basil is a special case and deserves at least cursory mention. Clearly a multitalented woman, she has worn many hats in her long entertainment career. Singer, dancer, actress, choreographer, and a director of music videos—all of these jobs are on her resumé. Her work on such classic early TV variety shows as *Shindig* and *Hullabaloo* (you've got to wonder whether she and Anka knew each other back then) led to a gig choreographing for George Lucas when he went to put together his classic coming-of-age film, *American Graffiti*.

Even earlier, Basil had appeared as a naked, acid-tripping prostitute in the Dennis Hopper classic, *Easy Rider*. Are you beginning to get the feeling that everything in this book is somehow related? (Wait 'til we get to David Soul.) It was a long, long, long stretch for Basil to go from the ultimate rebel film to one of the fluffiest songs to hit America in the early eighties, era of the Teflon President.

In 1982, America was neck deep in fluff, with *Porky's* a big hit in theaters, and *Dallas* and *Dynasty* cleaning up on TV. The "valley girl" trend was mercifully brief, and we had to put up with such trifling number one singles as "I Love Rock 'n Roll" by Joan Jett & The Blackhearts, "Eye of the Tiger" by Survivor, "Maneater" by Hall & Oates, and, of course, Toni Basil's "Mickey."

You remember.

To the shame of America, "Hey Mickey" was a number one single. (Actually, it's kind of a fun song, a guilty pleasure if you will.) Strangely, it was also to be the peak of Basil's career in entertainment. Two more singles followed from that album: "Shoppin' From A to Z," which hit a ceiling at number seventy-seven, and "Over My Head," which barely scraped its way to number eighty-one, a dire sophomore slump for her music career, one that continues to this day.

Basil still works in various fields. In 1990, she appeared in the failed vampire musical comedy film (uh, yeah) *Rockula*, along with other musical celebrities, including Thomas Dolby ("She Blinded Me With Science") and, of all people, blues master Bo Diddley.

133

Toni Basil, star of *Easy Rider* and TV's *Hullabaloo* had a number one hit called "Mickey" in 1982.

BLUE SWEDE

In the aftermath of the tumultuous sixties, and the pain of the Vietnam war, much of the music of the seventies was of a style and emotional bent that lent itself to criticism then, and now. Superficial fluff, many called it, a nicer term than "garbage," to be sure. Of course, bands like Led Zeppelin, The Eagles, and Lynyrd Skynyrd achieved their greatest popularity in the seventies with music that is still avidly listened to today.

But arena rock bands were not the most common practitioners of music during that decade. In fact, it is hard to imagine an era with more one-hit-wonders. We need look no further than the Starland Vocal Band (see below) for the perfect example.

It was a unique time in music. Previously, rock had been the music of youth, and "pop" had been their parents' crooned standards. In the 1970s, pop and rock, while still very different, began to target the same audiences. Pop music wanted to forget the war, forget Watergate, forget it all and concentrate on sunny days, stolen kisses, and lost loves.

It was in this cultural milieu that Blue Swede first appeared. The group consisted of six Swedish musicians, and beyond that, there is little of interest regarding the band. That they did not become yet another on that long list of one-hit-wonders can only be considered a fluke. Of the four singles that landed on *Billboard*'s Hot 100 chart, two failed miserably and two were top ten hits. The third single, "Never My Love," made it as high as number seven.

134

Their first single, however, was a sensation and is not only the perfect example of seventies pop, but nearly a definition of it. Debuting on the charts in February 1974, "Hooked on a Feeling," raced to number one. But this wasn't just any B.J. Thomas cover. This version began, intriguingly enough, with a chorus of "Ooga-Chaka, Ooga-Chaka." It has been a staple of soft rock stations, and on warm and sunny summer days, even of some rock and R&B stations, for twenty years. The lyrics tell us all we need to know about the era: "I'm hooked on a feeling, I'm high on believing, that you're in love with me."

It was happy, innocent music whose youthful benevolence was sorely lacking in the music of the late sixties and much of the rock of the day. While many readers, of all ages, will be familiar with the song, a sort of Partridge Family sound-alike tune, I'm willing to bet that almost nobody will remember the follow-up release, from June, 1974 . . . "Silly Milly." And with good reason, for it topped out at a miserable number seventy-one on the charts, a precipitous fall of seventy positions for the band-of-the-moment.

A brief moment it was.

DEBBY BOONE

Just the mention of her name is enough to send a generation into giggling fits. Regardless of her talent, which we shall not argue here, Debby Boone was universally ridiculed by kids used to Zeppelin, and the stigma of her music was made even worse by the fact that their parents were buying her album. Still, her success, no matter how short-lived, cannot be denied.

Her father was Pat Boone, one of the most popular crooners of the late fifties, who appeared frequently on television and even made a couple of movies. Debby had been a gospel singer with her family, and later became known as a Christian performer. Her father was a major celebrity in his day, and some of his biggest hits had come from the theme songs for films. It was only appropriate, then, that when daughter Debby wanted to make her big break into music, she did it with the theme song to a movie.

Unfortunately, while her father had recorded songs for films such as *Exodus*, *Friendly Persuasion* (starring Gary Cooper), and *Anastasia* (starring Ingrid Bergman), Debby Boone performed the theme song to *You Light Up My Life*. The film, which concerned a young woman attempting to make it in show business, died an ignominious death at the box office and featured no "name" talent, in front of or behind the camera. In fact, the only reason that the film has not been completely forgotten today, strangely enough, is that the single was so incredibly successful for Boone.

"You Light Up My Life" was a tearjerker of a ballad. Released in September 1977, the song sped to number one and remained there an incredible *ten weeks*. Ten weeks! (Shame on you, America!) Boone's next single was "California," which made it halfway up the chart to number fifty before choking and dropping off altogether. After the extraordinarily uncommon success of her first single, "California" had to be a major disappointment, perhaps even embarrassment, for the singer. Her final single, "God Knows," made it only half as high again as the second, peaking at number seventy-four. In the grand tradition of the Starland Vocal Band, Debby Boone won the 1977 Grammy Award for Best New Artist and has not appeared on the Hot 100 chart since 1978.

To be fair to Boone, it was not only parents who listened to her hit single in the fall of 1977. We would be remiss if we did not note that the song also became an anthem, of sorts, and for a very brief period, for all those teenybopper, puppy love couples whose entire world was each other, though they never would have admitted that, or their appreciation of the song, to their friends.

THE BYRDS

Folk, and folk-rock, is a musical form that has all but disappeared from the ranks of charted popular music. Thirty years ago, however, when The Byrds

Debby lit up our lives at number one for ten weeks in 1977. Can you name her second song? *Copyright ©1978 Columbia Pictures Industries, Inc.*

made their debut, it was one of the hottest types of music on the market. And The Byrds were one of the best known folk-rock bands in America. The original lineup of the Los Angeles–based group included David Crosby and Jim (Roger) McGuinn on guitars, Gene Clark and Michael Clarke on percussion and drums, respectively, and Chris Hillman on bass.

Each of the group's members had already achieved some small success before The Byrds. McGuinn, for instance, had worked with Bobby Darin, and Gene Clark had been a member of the New Christy Minstrels. Together, they had already recorded under the names The Jet Set and The Beefeaters (without Hillman and Clarke), but it was with The Byrds that they had their first real taste of fame. It was July 1965, and the album was called *Mr. Tambourine Man*. It climbed as high as number six. But two months earlier, the album's first single, of the same name, had hit radio and spent a total of thirteen weeks on the chart, one in the number one position. The combination of tight vocal harmonies and smooth guitars piqued the interest of America.

Their second release, two months later, was another Bob Dylan called "All I Really Want to Do" and rose to only number forty before dropping off again. While this still qualifies as a top forty single, and could perhaps be considered a hit by some, coming, as it did, on the heels of a number one debut single like "Mr. Tambourine Man," a forgotten song like "All I Really Want to Do" was a major disappointment to a group of guys who hard worked long and hard to finally make it.

Apparently disheartened regarding the hit prospects from what remained of their first album, The Byrds next single release came in advance of what would be their second album, *Turn, Turn, Turn*. The title track spent three weeks at number one in late 1965 and was one of the more unique number one songs of that or any era in that its lyrics had been taken by writer Pete Seeger, albeit somewhat altered, from the Bible, the Book of Ecclesiastes, chapter 3, verses 1 through 8.

The slight disappointment of "All I Want to Do" behind them thanks to the huge success of "Turn, Turn, Turn," The Byrds released their fourth single, both sides of which charted but neither of which rose higher than number sixty-three. Though they recorded several more top forty hits, The Byrds never again made the top ten. I feel compelled to note that in 1969, The Byrds hit the Hot 100 with the "Ballad of Easy Rider," the theme from that film, which seems to keep popping up.

The members of The Byrds left, individually and in groups, to pursue other endeavors and reunited several times. In various combinations they have been members of, or made up the entirety of, several other bands. The most successful of these efforts include bassist Chris Hillman's founding of country favorite, The Desert Rose Band, and, of course, David Crosby's efforts as a member of Crosby, Stills & Nash. Interestingly, though CSN had a string of top forty hits, and two top tens, they never hit number one. Hard to believe, but true—Crosby's only number ones are still those two he had with The Byrds.

McGuinn continued to record and perform, often with Hillman or Crosby. In 1991, his first real solo album, *Back From Rio*, was a middling hit, climbing to number forty-four on the *Billboard* 200 Album chart. A single, "King of the Hill," went to number two on the Album Rock Tracks chart, but failed to chart on the Hot 100. The album featured musical support from Elvis Costello and Tom Petty, as well as McGuinn's old Byrd-mates, Crosby and Hillman.

GENE CHANDLER

1962 was one of the most volatile years in American history. The nation put a human being in orbit around the Earth. The Cuban Missile Crisis had the world holding its breath. Marilyn Monroe died after a drug overdose, leading to decades of speculation about her sex life and whispers of conspiracy.

But 1962 was a transitional year in our culture, and music, which reflects the current feeling and mood of society, had not yet caught up with the times. Anger and fear had not yet infiltrated pop, and, instead, we had number ones like Little Eva's "The Loco-Motion," Shelley Fabares' "Johnny Angel," and the Four Seasons' "Big Girls Don't Cry." Gene Chandler, The Duke of Earl, fit right in.

The story of Chandler's biggest hit is a fascinating music industry anecdote. The R&B singer hailed from Chicago, and just before spending time overseas courtesy of the U.S. military, he had joined a singing group called the

Dukays. Upon his return, the group recorded for Nat Records, and then for Vee-Jay Records. But when their first single, "Duke of Earl" (you remember it, "Duke, Duke, Duke, Duke of Earl"), was to be released, a conflict arose with Nat Records regarding the group. Such conflicts had become commonplace in the industry years before and were still a frequent event. Wheeling and dealing, and stealing, were a lot easier when performers had one or two representatives rather than the army of managers, agents, lawyers, publicists, etc. they have today.

Previously known as Eugene Dixon, The Dukays' leader changed his named to Gene Chandler, and it was under that name that Vee-Jay released "Duke of Earl," in January 1962. So, in truth, Gene Chandler's first solo release, and the biggest hit of his long career, was recorded while he was with his former group, the Dukays. The Chandler-less Dukays had two songs hit the Hot 100 in the early sixties, but neither was much of a hit. (You've got to wonder what ever happened to those guys.)

Chandler was another story. He had several other top forty hits over the course of nearly two decades and a score of other charting singles. Unfortunately, after "Duke of Earl," he never returned to the top ten, and certainly not the number one position.

Gene Chandler's sophomore slump occurred two months after he had achieved overnight celebrity with his number one single (which had stayed at the top for three weeks). In light of how soon the next single came, and the similarity of the song's titles, it is truly amazing that "Walk On With the Duke" reached its plateau at number ninety-one, a drop rivaled by few others in this history of the charts. On the other hand, it could be that the similarity and the speed of the release worked against the singer's follow-up. In fact, it would be two years before Chandler had another top forty hit, with "Just Be True."

For several years, in the early seventies, Gene Chandler ran his own record label. In his ode to the music and culture of his youth, "Keepin' the Faith," Billy Joel hinted at the significance of Chandler's first single with the line, "And I thought I was the Duke of Earl, when I made it with a red head girl in a Chevrolet."

In 1962, Gene Chandler was hip.

CUTTING CREW

By the time this British band dropped in on America with its album *Broadcast*, in 1987, the line between rock and pop had all but disappeared. In the early nineties, with the birth of the Seattle Sound and the popularity of such bands as Nirvana, Pearl Jam, and Stone Temple Pilots, the line between rock and pop was redrawn, with a number of former rock stars now firmly entrenched on the pop side. But back in 1987, the two had merged so completely that Cutting Crew could be considered a rock band.

Their first single, which debuted on the charts in March 1987 and spent two weeks at number one, was "(I Just) Died in Your Arms." It was a time when national pride had been puffed up by a Teflon President's caution-to-the-wind measures, only to be smeared by the Iran-Contra hearings; when the reality of AIDS was just beginning to truly hit home, but Gary Hart and Jim Bakker were ruined by sex scandals; and when Wall Street allowed people to admit that they thought "greed (was) good," only to find an October week that was the worst stock market crisis in decades.

Gone and forgotten: 1987's Cutting Crew. *Photo credit: Knut Bry.*

It was a time of superficial satisfaction, with ugliness and fear lurking just beneath the surface. America needed the kind of escapism that had always been offered by pop music. Cutting Crew was among the many bands who offered that escape. While the seventies were chock full of one-hit-wonders, the late eighties featured the emergence of a number of musical acts who produced one, reasonably successful album and then vanished. Examples from 1987 include Club Nouveau, Gregory Abbott, Georgia Satellites, and Robbie Nevil—none ever released a second collection of tunes. Bands like Crowded House and, yes, Cutting Crew, did attempt follow-up albums, but with little or no success.

Three months after "(I Just) Died in Your Arms" went to number one, Cutting Crew released its second single, titled "One for the Mockingbird." The song climbed just inside the top forty, to number thirty-eight, before tumbling down. Sandwiched between the band's first hit and their third release, a number nine song called "I've Been in Love Before," it isn't surprising that few people today can recall "One for the Mockingbird," even though its release was not even a decade ago.

RICK DEES

A full year before the world would come down with *Saturday Night Fever*, America was already under attack by the "Disco Duck." A little-known disc jockey from Memphis, Tennessee, Rick Dees was twenty-six years old when his silly, catchy single, "Disco Duck (Part 1)" went to number one on *Billboard*'s Hot 100 chart. Perhaps the popularity of the song, which spent twenty-five weeks on the Hot 100, was due to its profound lyrics. "Disco, disco duck. Don't be a cluck. Disco duck."

Then again, perhaps not.

In any case, the song was incredibly, inexplicably popular, and it turned Dees and his "Cast of Idiots" into an overnight sensation. Disco had already begun to take the world by storm—the days when stadiums would be home to bonfires built with disco records were far off—and any song with the word *disco* in it was a hit. But how to guarantee a number one? Obviously, add a small, feathered, web-footed avian creature.

Nearly twenty years later, we still don't know what the hell a "Disco Duck" is, and it's not much of a stretch to imagine that Dees doesn't either. Even more of an endangered species, however, was the title animal in Dees's next single, "Dis-Gorilla (Part 1)." Only five months after his "overnight success," Dees could not get his second single higher than number fifty-six on the chart. We'll probably never know whether this was due to the quality of the song, or that dancing animals had lost their allure to your average American.

Dees never released a "Part 2" to either song, but in 1984, his third single, "Eat My Shorts," struggled to number seventy-five before disappearing. Though his recording career has apparently been abandoned, Dees has remained a celebrity, and a popular disc jockey, for nearly two decades. In 1984 he worked for one season as the host of TV's *Solid Gold*, a post held at various times by such talent as Dionne Warwick, Marilyn McCoo, and Andy Gibb. Serious company for the man who sent "Disco Duck" to the top of the charts.

In 1990, Dees, who had long since become a DJ in Los Angeles, received his own ABC television series called *Into the Night With Rick Dees*. A classic variety show, *Into the Night* featured musical performances, stand-up comedy, comedy sketches, and a classy house band, Billy Vera and the Beaters (who had their own number one hit in 1986 with "At This Moment"). Nevertheless, nobody tuned in to this midnight show. Spanning the decline of Carson and the rise of Letterman, who would? Dees was dropped when the show began its second year, and by November 1991, *Into the Night* had come to an end.

Dees, however, has always had his career as a disc jockey to fall back on. Like his associates and competitors, Casey Kasem and Shadoe Stevens, Dees has his own weekly nationally syndicated pop countdown show. Unlike Stevens, who uses *Billboard*'s charts, and Kasem, who uses those of *Radio & Records*, Dees and his company make up their own countdown. Makes one wonder where he might place "Disco Duck" on his own, personal chart.

BOBBIE GENTRY

The multimedia success enjoyed by Bobbie Gentry, based upon one hit song, has rarely been matched. Gentry, whose real name is Roberta Streeter, was born and raised in Mississippi, where she learned to play many different instruments, including guitar, banjo, and piano. Later, she moved to California, where she was living when she hit it big with "Ode to Billie Joe."

It was August 1967 when Bobbie Gentry's first single spent four weeks at number one on the Hot 100 and also made it to the top of the country chart. Three months later, her second single, "Okolona River Bottom Band," was only able to climb as high as number fifty-four. By her third single, "Louisiana Man," which barely squeaked onto the chart at number one hundred, Gentry's early success might have been a dim memory. And for most artists, it would have been.

Fortunately, Gentry's greatest successes came on the country chart, including several hits she recorded with Glen Campbell. So, though she had only three more top forty hits, the highest of which peaked at number twenty-seven, Gentry continued to be a big star in country music. She received the Best New Artist Grammy for 1967, based on the crossover success of "Ode to Billie Joe," and had her own, albeit short-lived, television series in the United Kingdom. In 1974, *The Bobbie Gentry Show* (aka *Bobbie Gentry's Happiness*) had an embarrassing four-week run on American television, thanks to CBS.

The 1976 film, *Ode to Billy Joe* (note the spelling change), which featured Robby Benson as a teenage boy who commits suicide rather than face his own questions about his homosexual feelings and one such experience.

147

Fellow Sophomore Slumpers Bobbie Gentry and Lorne Greene appear together in "Highlights of the Ice Capades 1970." Who could forget? *Copyright © 1970 NBC.*

While Gentry's song never specified what made Billie Joe jump, this seemed a stretch. Still, it did not bomb in theaters, and both the original and a newly recorded version of the song charted in July of that year.

LORNE GREENE

This perennial American father figure was actually a native of Canada. Born in 1914, he began his entertainment career as a radio newsman in the 1940s. In the fifties, he appeared in supporting roles in a string of popular films, including *Silver Chalice*, *Autumn Leaves*, *Peyton Place*, and *The Buccaneer*. Still, after nearly two decades as an entertainer, Greene's big break came in September 1959, with the debut of *Bonanza*.

Bonanza was the story of a wealthy widower named Ben Cartwright and his three sons, Adam, "Hoss," and Little Joe. the tale of their trails and tribulations, loves and losses, on the thousand-acre Ponderosa Ranch, lasted for fourteen incredible years as one of television's favorite programs. For ten straight years, *Bonanza* was in the top ten, and for three of those years, the show was number one.

It was during that time in 1964, that Lorne Green turned to music, sort of. Relying on the success of *Bonanza*, the actor released an album entitled *Welcome to the Ponderosa*. The album went to number thirty-five, and the first single, "Ringo," went all the way to number one, an incredible feat for a song with no singing. That's right. Greene used that deep, commanding voice to captivate America without singing a word—instead, he spoke the entire song. "Ringo" was one of only two spoken word recordings to reach the number one position in the rock era. (The other, for you true trivia hounds, was "Big Bad John," by Jimmy Dean, which spent five weeks at number one in December 1961 and January 1962.)

"Ringo" was a sensation. Strangely, and certainly qualifying the actor for sophomore slump status, his second single was released three months later to almost universal indifference. The song, entitled "The Man," spent only three weeks on the chart, and rose to only number seventy-two before disappearing. Greene never appeared on the Hot 100 again.

149

A musical career in his past, the actor continued his work on screens both big and small. Amazingly, Lorne Greene appeared on prime time television for twenty-seven straight years without interruption, from 1959 to 1986. After *Bonanza* was finally dropped in 1973, he did a short-lived detective drama called *Griff*. The following year, when Greene also appeared in the film *Earthquake*, he began a successful syndicated program called *Lorne Green's Last of the Wild*, a documentary series presenting endangered species in their wilderness settings. That program ran until 1979, but during its tenure, Greene also appeared on television in *Roots* and began starring in a huge-budget network science-fiction show called *Battlestar Galactica*.

In 1978, in the wake of the popularity of *Star Wars* the year before, ABC launched the most expensive television series produced up to that time. The same year, a film of the same title was released with all the major cast members, Greene chief among them. In 1979, the series changed its look and locale, but failed to attract any new viewers and was canceled. In 1981, he appeared in a short-lived series about firefighters, entitled *Code Red*, and then from 1982 to 1986, hosted another syndicated animal show, *Lorne Greene's New Wilderness*.

In 1987, Lorne Greene appeared in a TV movie called *The Alamo: Thirteen Days to Glory*. He died of a heart attack later that same year.

INTERLUDE

David Soul

MUSIC

Best known as Hutch on the television series *Starsky & Hutch*, Soul has the distinction of being the only person eligible to appear in two separate sections of this book, hence this special interlude. In truth, he began his career as a singer, appearing from time to time on the old *Merv Griffith Show*, with a ski mask over his head! Sort of like the Unknown Comic, but with music.

The Chicago native found fame on television, but halfway through the successful run of *Starsky & Hutch*, he also tried to follow his musical aspirations. In January 1977, he released one of the sappiest ballads of all time, "Don't Give Up on Us (Baby)." The song went straight to number one and confirmed the feelings of young women throughout the nation. While boys typically favored Starsky (Paul Michael Glaser) for his machismo, women were more likely to look toward the soulful Hutch for inspiration. The song was just icing on the cake.

The album, *David Soul*, did not debut until April and was able to squeeze into the fortieth position only with great difficulty. The following month, when Soul's second single, "Going in With My Eyes Open," was released, it limped as high as number fifty-four before dropping like a stone. A similar fate met "Silver Lady," the actor's third single, which barely snuck by its predecessor, to top out at fifty-two.

Soul's career as a singer lasted for almost exactly one year, destroyed by the abysmal performance of the releases that followed his first single.

TELEVISION

The Chicago native found fame on *Starsky & Hutch*. Soul played Ken Hutchinson, a police detective whose blonde, blue-eyed looks and quiet intelligence had the show's female fans swooning. Of course, series like *Starsky &*

Hutch are generally made for male audiences, and so many fans favored the harsher, dark-haired Starsky (played by Paul Michael Glaser).

They hit the mean streets of the city together in their bright red, racing striped Ford Torino, dealing with the roughest of the rough trade, pimps and drug dealers, thugs, and gangsters. Their chief snitch, and a character fondly recalled by fans of the show, was a less than law-abiding fellow named, uhm-hm, Huggy Bear. Ably played by Antonio Fargas, Huggy offered some of the show's best comic relief, and nearly locked the actor into a string of similar roles for the length of his career, at least as of this writing.

Starsky & Hutch first aired in September 1975 and ran for four seasons on ABC, shorter than most network hits. Though it made the top twenty-five only in its first year, finishing sixteenth, it was yet another series to spawn an incredible flood of licensed products, including toy cars based on that flashy Torino and, of course, lunchboxes. It also made stars of both Glaser and Soul. While the former went on to become a successful motion picture director, the latter continued in television.

While he would go on to star in numerous TV movies and miniseries of varying success (including the 1979 four-hour adaptation of Stephen King's *Salem's Lot*), Soul's next major TV project was another series, the undertaking of which must have required a plethora of guts, or a shortfall of brains. In April 1983, Soul starred as Rick Blaine in TV's second series based on the classic Humphrey Bogart film, *Casablanca*. The story of an American running a nightclub in North Africa, the series featured Soul in the Bogart role, solving other people's problems and attempting to subvert the Nazi cause. The greatest assets of the series were its supporting cast, including Hector Elizondo as Louis, Ray Liotta as Sacha, and Scatman Crothers as Sam the piano player.

After its initial release in April, *Casablanca* was on hiatus until August, only to be pulled again the following month. An utter failure. Soul must have been prepared for it, because it was just a month later, in October 1983, when he began to appear in *The Yellow Rose*, a modern-day western soap that also featured Sam Elliott, Cybill Shepherd, and Chuck Connors. The series ran off and on at NBC for seven months, but couldn't seem to garner an audience.

David Soul, Ray Liotta, and Hector Elizondo in NBC-TV's ill-fated show *Casablanca* Copyright © 1983 NBC.

Five years later, Soul returned for his fourth prime time network series, and his third failure in a row, perpetuating his sophomore slump. Ahead of its time, *Unsub* featured Soul, M. Emmet Walsh, and *Adam-12*'s Kent McCord, and concerned a group of Justice Department shrinks investigating suspected cases of serial killers. *Unsub* lasted two and a half months.

A talented actor, we hope that David Soul's three strikes have not sent him out of the TV batting box for good.

154

KC & THE SUNSHINE BAND

Florida native Harry Casey was twenty-four years old when his band hit the big time. The "K.C." in KC & The Sunshine Band had joined with a bass player named Richard Finch, wrote a whole slew of songs, and become the undisputed king of disco in 1975. Casey and Finch wrote and produced all the group's music, and the backup band's roster changed regularly.

In an era where the sentiment "have a nice day" took on profound meaning for a generation, when the most popular television programs in America were *Happy Days* and *Laverne & Shirley*, when pet rocks were all the rage, and when a peanut farmer from Georgia could be elected President of the United States, the happy, lighthearted hits of KC & The Sunshine Band were the perfect soundtrack. Every high school dance and pool party "got down" with Harry Casey and his cronies.

The band's first single to reach the Hot 100, "Get Down Tonight," debuted on the Hot 100 in the heat of July 1975. With the bicentennial celebration just around the corner, the Watergate criminals culled from the Washington herd, and the unresolved questions about Vietnam still kept in the shadows, America was beginning to feel proud of itself again. People wanted to dance. "Get Down Tonight" went to number one.

For kids and teens, especially, the radio is everything. Their lives are defined, outlined, perpetuated by the music of their time. It's fascinating to talk with people who fondly, though often guiltily, remember the heyday of their youth in the mid-seventies, when KC & The Sunshine Band were a part of the sound track. In the memories of those "kids," KC had one hit after another, with none more closely linked than the first two, "Get Down Tonight" and "That's The Way (I Like It)" (*uh-huh, uh-huh*), both number ones.

But that isn't how it happened. "That's The Way (I Like It)" actually hit the charts a full three months

KC and The Sunshine Band let Frankie Valli sing along on "New Years Rockin' Eve 1977." *Copyright © 1977 ABC.*

155

later than "Get Down Tonight." In between, in early September 1975, KC & The Sunshine Band released "Shotgun Shuffle." Sandwiched between two number ones, the failure of that single, which peaked at number eighty-eight and dropped off after only two weeks on the chart, is even more surprising. It is hard to explain, especially in a modern day when the title alone would ensure a number one hit for any gangsta' rapper looking to score with a cover version.

Interestingly, the phenomenon repeated itself between "That's The Way" and the group's next number one, "(Shake, Shake, Shake) Shake Your Booty." Long forgotten is the song that was released between them, "Queen of Clubs," which rose only as high as number sixty-six.

KC & The Sunshine Band, it seemed, were capable only of extremes. Again, after "Shake Your Booty" came "I Like to Do It," which barely squeaked into the top forty, and then the number one single "I'm Your Boogie Man."

Number one to number eighty-eight, back to number one then to number sixty-six, back to number one then to number thirty-seven, back to number one, and finally, the weird pattern was broken when the group's eighth single, "Keep It Comin' Love" spent three weeks at number two.

But then it was all over. Two years would pass before KC would rise higher than number thirty-five. In 1979, they scored a number one and a number two hit, then dropped out of sight. A comeback effort in 1983 was rewarded with one top twenty single, but nothing worthy of more than a footnote. The days of pet rocks, nice days, and disco music were over, and so were the days of KC & The Sunshine Band, though Harry Casey has recently announced his intention to get the band back on the road.

Who knows? Nostalgia can be a powerful sales tool. Ask The Eagles.

THE KINGSTON TRIO

Widely considered to be the harbingers of the national fascination with folk music that lasted throughout the early sixties, this San Francisco–based group began their tenure on the Hot 100 in a big way, with "Tom Dooley." The song, which went to number one and spent twenty-one weeks on the charts, was a traditional American folk song and an instant hit for the group.

Four months later, their second single, "Raspberries, Strawberries," reached only number seventy. While they had several top twenty hits, it would be five years before they would sneak back into the top ten with "Reverend Mr. Black," a number eight single.

On the other hand, it is important to note that while the group's singles never again achieved the popularity of "Tom Dooley," their albums continued to do extraordinarily well. In fact, of their nineteen albums, five reached the number one position, collectively logging forty-six weeks there. Nine others made it into the top ten, and all but one into the top twenty. This more than anything else shows the influence and enduring popularity of The Kingston Trio.

One of the foremost folk groups in America, they appeared frequently on

157

the television programs of the day. However, like several other performers, including Peter, Paul & Mary and Joan Baez, they refused an invitation to appear on the program *Hootenanny* because the show (which aired during the 1963–64 television season) perpetuated the practice of blacklisting performers who were alleged to have certain liberal views.

After the group split up in 1968, guitarist Bob Shane formed the New Kingston Trio.

158

THE MARVELLETTES

The sixties were the golden age of girl groups in America. Only in recent years, with the emergence of such R&B acts as En Vogue and SWV have we seen the phenomenon even begin to move toward the heights it had reached in the early to mid sixties: The Supremes, The Chiffons, The Ronettes, Martha & The Vandellas, The Shirelles, and, of course, The Marvellettes. While they were perhaps not as well-known later on as some of their more enduring counterparts, in 1961, The Marvellettes were the hottest thing going.

In September of that year, The Marvellettes' first single, "Please Mr. Postman," began a twenty-three week run on the Hot 100, a march that would inexorably lead to the number one position. The song still inspires radio audiences to turn up the volume today. While their second single did not fall nearly as far as some of the other sophomore slumps, it is also valuable to illustrate a popular marketing move at the time.

Just as Gene Chandler flopped going from "Duke of Earl" to "Walk on With the Duke," so The Marvellettes also blew a startling debut by attempting to capitalize on their first single's success. The second single was "Twistin' Postman," a bizarre concept at best, and one that garnered them only the thirty-fourth slot on the Hot 100. While this is still top forty material, it is clear that their gimmick didn't work, a major disappointment after so promising a start. Though their third single, "Playboy," went to number seven, the Marvellettes had only one more top ten single in their career. Most of their later releases never made it into the top fifty.

One of the most interesting facets of the group's story, however, comes from their personal lives. The Michigan-based group was formed in 1960. Several years later, two of the women would marry members of popular male R&B groups of the day. Wanda Young was wed to Bobby Rogers of Smokey Robinson's group, the Miracles. Georgeanna Tillman, who died in 1980, married The Contours' Billy Gordon.

MAUREEN McGOVERN

This Ohio-born woman made a career for herself in the seventies by recording theme songs for movies and television programs. Interestingly, only two of her songs are still heard regularly on radio, one a huge hit and one a romantic flop. The former, "The Morning After," was her first single and spent two weeks at the top of the charts. It had the dubious distinction of being the love theme

Disaster movie diva Maureen McGovern.

from the film *The Poseidon Adventure*, though having seen the film, one must wonder what constitutes a love theme.

That was in June 1973, and a few months later, McGovern made a major wrong turn that would define the remainder of her recording career. Her second single, "I Won't Last a Day Without You," was not the theme from anything, and, consequently, despite McGovern's vocal abilities, it topped out at a dismal eighty-ninth position on the Hot 100 chart.

Of course, being a theme song wasn't a guarantee of success, as the vocalist discovered with her third single, the theme from the film *Cinderella Liberty*, "Nice To Be Around." Of course, it helps if the film is a success as well, but in any case, "Nice To Be Around" bubbled under at number 101 for four weeks, but never made it onto the Hot 100. Even the song she recorded for *The Towering Inferno*, in which she had a role, only made it to number eighty-three.

Fortunately, McGovern had greater success with her final two singles. In February 1979, she released the love theme from the film *Superman*, called

160

"Can You Read My Mind." Though the song never got as far as the top half of the chart, it is remembered by many, and still played on some radio stations today. McGovern's last single was the theme from the TV series *Angie*, starring Donna Pescow and Robert Hays. Though the show lasted only one season, McGovern managed to slip into the top twenty with the song "Different Worlds," which climbed to number eighteen and spent sixteen weeks on the chart.

McGovern is also known for her work in musical theater. She starred in *Pirates of Penzance* on Broadway. Many of us, however, will remember her best as the sweetly wacky, guitar-playing nun, Sister Angelina, in the film *Airplane*. Everybody, watch your IV tubes!

MILLI VANILLI

At a time when major acts from Madonna to Janet Jackson to New Kids on the Block were being accused of lip-synching in concert, even the suggestion of which sent music audiences into contortive fits of anger and disgust, one of the most incredibly audacious scams of all time

161

Who needs talent? The notorious Milli Vanilli.

was hatched by music producer Frank Farian and two arrogant European poseurs named Rob Pilatus and Fab Morvan.

While vocalists Charles Shaw, John Davis, and Brad Howe were paid to record an album of music, Farian went about the heady business of making Pilatus and Morvan into international pop superstars, on the strength of the other artists' recordings, under the name Milli Vanilli. It was an incredible hoax, deliberately perpetrated on the public, and it spawned five top ten singles in a row, including three number ones, before the lid was blown off the whole thing.

"Girl You Know It's True," "Baby Don't Forget My Number," "Girl I'm Gonna Miss You," "All or Nothing," and "Blame It on the Rain" were huge hits from the album *Girl You Know It's True*. The pair were media darlings, and even Grammy fell under their spell when they received the award for Best New Artist of 1989. While the category has often been home to sophomore slump candidates and one-hit-wonders, including Starland Vocal Band and Debby Boone, this was an entirely different story.

When the worldwide deception was discovered, the National Academy of Recording Arts & Sciences demanded that Pilatus and Morvan return their Grammy, the only time NARAS has ever taken such an action. The pair embarrassed themselves further while trying to prove to international press that they could indeed sing. How did they embarrass themselves? Just as I said . . . they sang.

Their album, *Girl You Know It's True*, was an extraordinary success, and one of the most popular albums of 1989. It spent sixty-one weeks on the *Billboard* 200 Albums chart and an enviable eight weeks at number one. What is perhaps most fascinating about this particular sophomore slump is that it occurred before Milli Vanilli was exposed as a fraud.

The Remix Album, more than half of which was exactly that—remixes from their first album—was released in June 1990 and did not break into the top thirty. Though successful by the standards of most artists, after *Girl You Know It's True*, this was a major disappointment. Milli Vanilli's sophomore slump would become a forever slump when the group's duplicity was revealed later in November. Though Rob & Fab have threatened to release their own album for some time, it has yet to materialize.

SINEAD O'CONNOR

She burst onto the scene as the darling of music journalists around the world. Her quirky facets, including that shaved pate, were just a part of her allure, the delicate Irish flower

2 Much 2 Soon? Sinead O'Connor wore out her welcome real fast.

163

turned rebellious. In short order she became an international superstar. But it seemed an impossible task for her to fulfill the requirements for that job. Her tales of a hellish childhood began as sympathetic and eventually became merely odd.

It all began with her debut album, *The Lion and the Cobra*, in February 1988. Though O'Connor did not appear on the Hot 100 chart at all in support of this album, it still was able to make it to number thirty-six on the *Billboard* 200 Albums chart—quite a feat. However, it was with her second album, *I Do Not Want What I Haven't Got*, that O'Connor reached superstar status. The album went quickly to number one and spent a full year on the chart. Conversely, her third album, *Am I Not Your Girl?*, rose only as high as number twenty-seven and spent only nine weeks on the *Billboard* 200. By that time, her antics had already gotten Sinead O'Connor in too deep.

The first single from *I Do Not Want What I Haven't Got*, "Nothing Compares 2 U," was written by Prince and went from its debut spot at number sixty-three to the top position in five weeks, reaching number one in April 1990. O'Connor's sophomore slump began with the release of her second single from that album, "The Emperor's New Clothes." Only three months after she took the world by storm, her second single barely made its way to number sixty on the Hot 100.

The slump continued as O'Connor's behavior became less and less palatable to the American public. She refused to perform if the U.S. national anthem was played before her show, a common practice at many musical venues. Public comments and actions continued to take their toll, until, at last, O'Connor put the final nail in the coffin of her career. While performing as a musical guest on *Saturday Night Live* to promote the release of *Am I Not Your Girl?*, O'Connor held up a photograph of Pope John Paul II. "Fight the real enemy," she said as she tore it to shreds.

Way to make friends and gain fan support, Sinead! Though O'Connor was obviously reacting to her upbringing and the troubled state of her mind at that time, few members of the television audience could understand her message while being assaulted by such an offensive gesture. Whether she will ever recover from such an incident is unknown, but her prospects seem dim. Recent appearances and performances, including her stint with Roger Daltrey and his "Daltrey Sings Townshend" tour, have met with booing from the audience.

THE OSMONDS

Perhaps no musical act better personified the "let's get happy" school of pop in the 1970s than The Osmonds, in all their various groupings. During the previous decade, the four oldest brothers in the "world's most famous Mormon family" worked together as a barbershop quartet. They appeared regularly as The Osmond Brothers on *The Andy Williams Show*, from 1962 to 1971, joined from time to time by various other family members. Little brother Donny made his debut on December 10, 1963, at the tender age of six.

It was just over seven years later that The Osmonds made their record-

Those musical Mormons, The Osmond Brothers, Alan, Merril, Jay, and Wayne.

ing debut with a self-titled album, which rose to number fourteen on the charts. The five brothers were talented, but as with another singing family, all eyes were on the child prodigy. Donny was thirteen years old when their first single, "One Bad Apple," hit the charts in January 1971. The song was immensely popular, spending five weeks at number one, and was such a hit that people commonly credit it to the Jacksons (who are widely held to have had far more talent than their Mormon counterparts).

After all those years on television, the Osmonds were a sensation. Which makes it all the more incredible that their second single, released only two months after "One Bad Apple," was one of the biggest sophomore slumps in the history of music. The song was called "I Can't Stop," and it spent an appalling, embarrassing one week on the chart, at number ninety-six. What a disappointment that must have been, especially for young Donny, the new heartthrob to America's teeny-boppers.

Fortunately, their luck turned around with the next single, "Double Lovin'," almost as if the words to "One Bad Apple" had come true. The third single went to number fourteen. Though The Osmonds never had another number one, they put two later singles in the top five, and only two of their subsequent releases failed to make the top forty.

While The Osmonds, minus Donny, went on to have a successful career as a country act, several other family members also had musical careers. Donny had always been a solo artist, recording such teenybopper hits as "Puppy Love" and the number one "Go Away Little Girl." In fact, after more than twenty years off the charts, Donny Osmond returned in 1989 to score a number two single called "Soldier of Love."

The youngest member of the family, Little Jimmy Osmond, also performed separately, as did sister Marie, who scored a top five hit in 1973 with "Paper Roses." From 1976 to 1979, Donny and Marie had their own variety show, aptly titled *Donny and Marie*. She was "a little bit country," and he was "a little bit rock and roll," but somehow they made it all work. It was a real family show and popular with kids. The hosts were eighteen and sixteen, respectively, and that may have been much of the appeal.

The other Osmonds appeared regularly on the program, and, in fact, from January 1979 until its cancellation in May, the title was changed to *The Osmond Family Show*. Donny and Marie had a half dozen top forty hits together, with two in the top ten, and Marie went on to become a very popular country music star in the eighties. In fact, in 1980, she had her own, very short-lived variety show, *Marie*, and from 1985 to 1986, she cohosted *Ripley's Believe It or Not*. Currently, Marie Osmond is starring in the traveling company of the revived *The Sound of Music*, as Maria Von Trapp.

Sorry, Marie. Julie Andrews you ain't.

STARLAND VOCAL BAND

While we have tried to shy away from musical acts that are one-hit-wonders, unless they have some other significance such as film or television careers, we must make an exception for one of the most notorious one-hit-wonders of all time, Starland Vocal Band. (Actually, the band's inclusion was in question, until we ran across one spectacular piece of trivia, which we'll get to in a moment.)

It was the summer of 1976, the bicentennial year. The beaches of America were packed with people humming one song, the ultimate beach song.

Happy, superficial, and just-damn-glad-to-be-alive could have described the song or the people themselves. For kids who were on the beach that summer, the first release by Starland Vocal Band has almost surreally etched itself into memory as if it were the only song played by disc jockeys for the entire season. And maybe it was.

The song, of course, was "Afternoon Delight." The strains of its chorus were perfect for the bicentennial Fourth of July, as the group sang of "skyrockets in flight." The song was the ultimate in pop trash, a rockable, singalongable, radioblarable paean to summer lovin'. But what the heck, it was one song. Sure, it hit number one, but the band's follow-up, "California Day," made it to only number sixty-six. Their only other two charting singles tied at number seventy-one.

What is most extraordinary about "Afternoon Delight," however, is how far it took Starland Vocal Band. Incredibly, they won the Grammy Award for Best New Artist of 1976. But perhaps more importantly, for the entire summer of 1977, America was blessed with *The Starland Vocal Band Show* on CBS. And no, I'm not kidding. You may not remember it, but it was there. It was a variety show that included musical performances and comedy skits, as well as political satire by the popular Mark Russell (what was he thinking?).

And here's that bit of trivia. Several members of the program's writing staff actually performed in the comedy sketches they wrote. One of those writer-comedians, a regular on *The Starland Vocal Band Show*, was a young guy named

Dave Letterman. Uh-huh. Dave Letterman. So, if you ever have an opportunity to meet our TV friend Dave, please be sure to remind him of this early triumph.

A TASTE OF HONEY

It was the summer of 1978, and A Taste of Honey climbed to the top of the charts with the quintessential disco song, "Boogie Oogie Oogie." (I'm telling you, that's the title. If you don't believe me, look it up.)

"If you think you're too cool to boogie," the song went, "boy, oh boy have I got news for you."

No, really, I'm serious. "Boogie Oogie Oogie" spent three weeks at number one, twenty-three weeks total on the Hot 100. And on the *strength* of that fabulous first effort (and we wonder what inspired the vinyl bonfires of the late seventies–early eighties?), the National Academy of Recording Arts & Sciences gave A Taste of Honey the Grammy for Best New Artist of 1978!

Aaaarrrggghhh! Another one. Milli Vanilli, Starland Vocal Band, Debby Boone, Bobbie Gentry. Will the list never end? What were *they* thinking? In any case, unlike the SVB or Miss Boone, A Taste of Honey did have a second top ten hit. In 1981, "Sukiyaki" went to number three. Before that, however, their second single, "Do It Good," limped its way to number seventy-nine before disappearing forever, narrowly averting the destruction of the world as we know it!

Come on, now. "Boogie Oogie Oogie?"

Please!

170

VANILLA ICE

White rap had been done before, most memorably by The Beastie Boys, but no white musical artist had entered into the rap arena with the attitude of Vanilla Ice. Attitude was, and still is in many cases, half of what it takes to make it as a rap star. So here he was, this skinny little white guy with a really bad haircut and a sneer worthy of Billy Idol, breaking into rap music by harshing on his competitors, including the number one rapper of the day, M.C. Hammer (and whatever happened to that guy?).

Vanilla Ice sweeps Kristin Minter off her feet in his movie debut, *Cool As Ice*.
Copyright © 1991 Universal City Studios Inc. All rights reserved.

171

Ice's real name is Robert Van Winkle (I couldn't possibly make that up). Born and raised in Florida, he claimed to have had a gang background, which seemed difficult to substantiate. Truth or not, it became clear at that point that having experience in the kind of life rappers typically represent was often far more important that having the talent to do it well.

Vanilla Ice was not making friends fast. Despite the fact that his first album, *To The Extreme*, was a number one hit, his arrogance was quickly turning many in the media against him, not to mention some fans. In fact, his claims about his past were in quite a bit of doubt, hastening comparisons to movie star Steven Seagal, whose assertions that he had worked with the CIA were also called into question. Fortunately for Seagal, his career has only continued to improve, but Ice started at the very top and slid rapidly down from there.

To The Extreme spent sixty-seven weeks on the chart and spawned two top ten singles, one of which, "Ice Ice Baby," hit number one. By the third single, he couldn't break into the top fifty. Vanilla Ice was, essentially, over. More evidence was forthcoming when the rapper's second album, *Extremely Live*, was released in July 1991. It just barely squeaked into the top thirty on the album chart. The one single released after that, "Cool As Ice," rose only as high as number eighty-one. So here, though his second single was a hit, we do count Ice's second album as his sophomore slump, the start of a long slumber for Rip Van Winkle's namesake.

"Cool As Ice," it is amusing to note, was the theme song from a movie by the same title, a starring vehicle for the rapper, meant to launch him into pop culture superstardom. Instead, the film about Ice's courtship of a young woman was a huge turkey, remarkable only for the fact that anybody would last the length of a film shoot working with an actor as bad as old R. Van Winkle. What Michael Gross, of TV's *Family Ties*, was doing in this film is anybody's guess. It comes as no surprise, and somewhat of a comfort, to learn that the film's director, David Kellogg, has apparently done nothing of note in the years since *Cool As Ice*, his first "big picture."

Ice recently released a new album, though it seems unlikely there were many people clamoring for such a move. Though not that far a fall from number one to number thirty, Ice's sophomore slump was only beginning then, and continues as of this writing. Despite the media coverage he is afforded as a fallen star, it seems unlikely that Ice, draped in dreadlocks and sporting a goatee, will ever return from slump-land.

BOBBY VINTON

This son of a Pennsylvania bandleader was a much loved balladeer as well as a Polish polka king with his own television show. From the band he formed in high school, Vinton went on to become a very successful solo artist beginning with the first, and biggest, single he ever released, "Roses Are Red (My Love)." The song spent four weeks at number one in 1962. The kind of love song Vinton quickly became known for had been around since the beginning of record-

174

O.J. Simpson, Jessica (*Play Misty for Me*) Walters, and Sophomore Slumper Bobby Vinton on BV's television show.

ed music and is still popular today, thought he singer has long since gone the way of Neil Sedaka.

Vinton's second single was not nearly as drastic a sophomore slump as some others in this book, but after four full weeks at number one, the disappointing showing of "I Love You the Way You Are," which rose only to number thirty-eight, barely inside the top forty, must have seemed a dismal second effort. Fortunately, he bounced back to number twelve with his third release, "Rain Rain Go Away," and yet Vinton would try several times more before returning to the top ten with "Blue On Blue," and then the number one spot with "Blue Velvet," the song that became his theme.

"Blue Velvet" spent three weeks at number one, and Vinton followed it up with another chart topper, "There I've Said It Again," which logged four weeks in the top slot. His final number one was "Mr. Lonely" in 1964, but Vinton continued to turn out top ten singles through the early seventies, when "Melody of Love," went to number three.

From 1975 to 1978, the singer hosted his own variety show in national syndication. A middling success, the show featured music, and comedy sketches by such veterans as Arte Johnson, Henny Youngman, and John Byner. With his almost afro-like curly locks and jumpsuits that would have impressed the King himself, Vinton was an unusual TV star—older viewers assumed he was "with it" and younger viewers considered him laughably unhip.

STEVIE WONDER

Born in Michigan in 1950, Steveland Morris would one day become Stevie Wonder, among the most beloved performers in the history of modern music.

Stevie Wonder rebounded quickly from his sophomore slump, "I Call It Pretty Music, But the Old People Call It the Blues."

Blind from birth, Wonder overcame his handicap to become an award-winning singer-songwriter and music producer, mastering many different musical instruments. Named "Little Stevie Wonder" by Berry Gordy Jr. when he began to record for Motown in the early sixties, the musical autuer also appeared in several films, including, dare we say it, *Muscle Beach Party*. Reflecting the music man's age at the time of the recording of his first album, it was entitled, *Little Stevie Wonder, The Twelve Year Old Genius*, and it was also his first number one album.

The first single off that album, "Fingertips, Part Two," enjoyed an enviable three weeks at number one, in the summer of '63, not bad for a pubescent musician. That single spent fifteen weeks on the chart. Incredibly, with the release of his next single, Stevie Wonder nearly became a one-hit-wonder pop chart casualty. The title of the song was "I Call It Pretty Music, But the Old People Call It the Blues, Part One," and it was an unmitigated disaster for the young man, the greatest sophomore slump in pop music.

Billboard magazine used to publish a chart called "Bubbling Under the Hot 100." The chart varied in length, the most common being fifteen positions. It represented the singles that were, as the title indicates, just under the one hundredth position and likely to make it to the Hot 100. Most didn't. One of those, incredibly, was "I Call It Pretty Music, But the Old People Call It the Blues, Part One," which is also (I believe) the longest song title in this book. The song spent one week in August of 1963 on the "Bubbling Under" chart, at the top, number 101, which means that Wonder bests Paul Anka's ninety-six position drop by making his own plummet an even one hundred positions.

His third single, "Workout, Stevie, Workout" fared better, rising to number thirty-three, and then Wonder was on his way, preparing for a long string of successes that would garner him nearly twenty Grammy Awards and twenty-seven top ten singles, including ten number ones. His top ten hits include "For Once in My Life," "My Cherie Amour," "Superstition," "You Are the Sunshine of My Life," "Living for the City," "Sir Duke," the duet with Paul McCartney "Ebony and Ivory," "I Just Called to Say I Love You," and "Part Time Lover."

Wonder had huge success with his albums as well, scoring ten top ten albums and three number ones. His greatest success came with 1976's *Songs in the Key of Life*, which spent a phenomenal fourteen weeks at number one. This is made all the more incredible by the fact that three years before Wonder had been in an automobile accident that almost took his life. After more than thirty years, Stevie Wonder remains one of the biggest stars in the history of popular music.

PART FOUR: TV STARS

It would have been so easy to do a whole book about sequels and spin-offs. But that would have been much too easy because, with few exceptions, TV sequels die lonely deaths based upon abysmal ratings. How many of us can really look back fondly on *AfterMASH*, *Golden Palace*, *The Tortellis*, *Joanie Loves Chachi*, *Flo*, *The Colbys*, *Tabitha*, *A Man Called Hawk*, or *Richie Brockelman, Private Eye*? No, we had to go with individual television actors.

So, the criteria? Like movie stars, the TV stars selected had to have been the male or female lead character in the program. Only prime time broadcast series, both network and nationally syndicated, were considered. As I explained in the Introduction, success or failure in other media was not considered, the evaluation of potential candidates based solely on their work in series television.

What follows are shows you remember fondly, barely, or not at all, good, bad, and really, really bad, and stories of bad luck, bad decisions, and bad acting that led to sophomore slump status.

VALERIE BERTINELLI

She was the girl-next-door who stole the hearts of prepubescent (and plenty of adolescent, I'll wager) boys across America. Though Bonnie Franklin and Mackenzie Phillips also starred on the show, it was really Bertinelli that everyone was watching. That perfect smile and those dimples charmed the hearts of America.

By any standards, *One Day at a Time* was typical sitcom fare. Franklin was the divorced mother of two girls, trying to start life anew while raising them as best she could. Phillips was the older sister and Bertinelli the younger, and their rivalry and boy troubles were a large portion of the show. Stir in a goofy building super, and *voila!* Instant sitcom. But sometimes *One Day at a Time* was more than that. More often that not, this was due to Franklin's performance rather than that of other cast members.

Still, with its combination of family humor and pathos, and the charm of its leads, the show managed to stay in the top twenty from its debut in December 1975 to 1983, the year before it went off the air.

Like *Bewitched* star Elizabeth Montgomery, both Phillips and Franklin would be in this book with Bertinelli except for one small problem . . . when their series ended in 1984, both stars completely disappeared from prime time episodic television. Phillips had a history of drug problems and had been thrown off the series twice. She later became a singer with her parents' former group, The Mamas & The Papas. Franklin? Who knows?

Bertinelli, on the other hand, had married Eddie Van Halen, whose band became *huge* in the eighties. The couple looked hauntingly similar, from the dimples and smile to the hair, and their marriage is one of those few Hollywood

Valerie Bertinelli's girl-next-door effervescence could not help *Sydney* from falling flat.

unions that seems destined to last. Bertinelli's role as Barbara Cooper on *One Day at a Time* had made her the darling of a nation. When she married Van

Halen, according to time-honored tabloid fashion, her reputation ought to have been tarnished by the rock and roll lifestyle. Interestingly, the opposite occurred. Van Halen became a regular guy, a real apple pie Americana type, regardless of the fact that he fronted one of the most popular musical acts of the day.

Goofy though it may have been, *One Day at a Time* helped to show young people across America that there were families that were not necessarily made up of Mom, Dad, 2.5 kids, and a dog. Conversely, even the most conservative viewers must have been comforted by the presence of Schneider as silly father figure. The best of both worlds. When the show centered on Bonnie Franklin's character, it had a lot to say about living in modern times.

Though she never had the success in later years that she did as Barbara Cooper, Bertinelli remains a star. A string of fairly successful TV movies have kept her in the public light, though both of her attempts at series television after *One Day at a Time* have failed miserably, making her into our first TV sophomore slump.

Her second effort, *Sydney*, featured Bertinelli as a struggling Los Angeles private investigator, in 1990, six years after her smash hit had gone off the air. Though Bertinelli was her engaging self, and her innocent appearance made the premise of the program amusing, it simply did not garner the following CBS apparently believed it would. Perhaps the two most interesting tidbits of information regarding the show are that it featured Daniel Baldwin, of the

Baldwin acting dynasty, as a sleazy bar patron who regularly hit on Bertinelli, and a theme song written by Eddie Van Halen and performed by the band.

During the 1993–1994 TV season, Bertinelli tried again, as an American woman running a business in France. The show, *Cafe Americain*, was cancelled before the season was even half over, and finished a dismal 103 out of 128 prime time series. Though she continues to work in television, and continues to be a popular celebrity due to her past success and her marriage to Van Halen, Bertinelli is still in the depths of a sophomore slump that has, at this point, lasted nearly a decade.

ROBERT BLAKE

Robert Blake had already appeared in a number of films, most notably *Tell Them Willie Boy Is Here* and *In Cold Blood*, when he moved to television. And, in fact, he may not have made the move at all had it not been for another actor, Tony Musante. Musante had been starring in a series called *Toma*, based on the real life of a rebellious Newark, New Jersey, cop named David Toma. Apparently unhappy with TV work, however, Musante left after the first season. The show was then retooled to allow a new star to take Musante's place as Toma. By the time the producers were done, they had their star, Robert Blake, but they had made so many changes that it wasn't Toma's story anymore, so they needed a new title to go with it.

Baretta.

The show was a modest hit, twenty-two in the ratings for its first year, but dropping out of the top twenty-five the year after that. Still, in certain demographics, *Baretta* was dynamite. Teamed in its first year with *Starsky & Hutch*, it was possibly the most violent night on television, and that at a time when *S.W.A.T.* was also on. (Congress sought to go back and look at the seventies, don't you think? Perhaps they can censor retroactively, so we don't remember these shows?)

Baretta's success was based on one, irrefutable fact. The show was cool. From the opening theme, "Keep Your Eye on the Sparrow," performed by Sammy Davis Jr., to Fred the cockatoo, who was often portrayed as Baretta's only confidant, to the dirty streets of the city, the show was cool. We know Baretta now, because we've seen a million like him. Even then, we'd seen a few. But Blake's stern face and empathetic acting put the audience right there with him. Whether he was prowling the street in his T-shirt, cap, and jeans, mouthing off to his boss, or busting some thug, heck, even when he was lying around his apartment philosophizing with that damn bird, we were with him.

The character of Baretta was a tough, rough, but beneath that veneer of hardheartedness, he was a benevolent soul. So after the program was cancelled, it was no surprise that the next series he starred in would also have that combination of machismo and morality. In *Hell Town*, Blake portrayed Father Noah Rivers, AKA Father "Hardstep." Actually, in its meager three months on the air, *Hell Town* seemed almost like one long under-cover assignment for Baretta, so similar were the personalities of the two characters. To top it all off, the theme song was again sung by Sammy Davis Jr.

But it was 1985, and *Baretta* was years gone by. Instead, Blake was portraying an ex-con turned priest who was determined to bring God's love and justice to East L.A., all at the same time. With corny tough-guy dialogue, the show just wasn't as believable as *Baretta*. After its final episode aired, on Christmas, Blake began a leave of absence from prime time series television that is still in effect. Whether that is by the actor's choice is a question yet unanswered, but Blake's sophomore slump, *Hell Town*, is long forgotten, and his triumph in Baretta still remembered fondly. Perhaps it's time to try again?

God knows in a TV market that includes one formerly successful actor after another turning up in clones of *Murder, She Wrote* and *Matlock*, we could use a truly tough television detective.

Robert Blake in *Hell Town*. Baretta's change of habit was too much for viewers. *Copyright © 1985 NBC.*

185

CHUCK CONNORS

Connors's long film career includes, surprisingly, very few highlights. Among them are 1957's *Old Yeller*, 1963's *Flipper*, and 1973's *Soylent Green*. Author Stephen King would add a little-seen 1979 horror film, *Tourist Trap*, to that list as well. Though King says, in his book *Danse Macabre*, that he enjoys the movie, he admits that Connors "isn't very good in the film . . . he's simply miscast," but goes on to say that the film is worth watching anyway.

Still, Chuck Connors will always be known as a television actor, for that is where he started and where he was ever the most visible. And as a television actor, he will always be known for *The Rifleman*. The actor, who had formerly made a living playing baseball, portrayed Lucas McCain, a rancher in the Old West, raising a young son on his own. McCain was well-known for his incredible dexterity with a rifle, and so the town's lawmen commonly called on him for assistance.

The Rifleman ran on ABC from 1958 to 1963, during the golden age of the TV western. In its first season, the show was fourth in the ratings, but dropped down to thirteenth in its second year, and out of the top twenty-five thereafter. Still, there is no denying that it was a successful program and made an acting career for a former ball player.

After completing *The Rifleman*, Connors began a sophomore slump that continued through his appearance in the Fox Network's *Werewolf* during its one

186

season run from 1987 to 1988. The actor starred in one failed series after another. First was *Arrest & Trial*, in which Connors starred with Ben Gazzara, and which, in essence, was the blueprint for the nineties series *Law & Order*. In fact, the two are so similar, it's a wonder the producers of the former did not receive credit and payment from those of the latter. Of course, *Arrest & Trial* lasted only one year.

Having bad luck playing a defense attorney in modern times, Connors next returned to the Old West in *Branded*, which ran during the 1965–1966 season. Still, there was little to compare this program to the role that made Connors famous. In *Branded*, he played Jason McCord, a West Point graduate and army captain wrongly dismissed from service due to a false charge of cowardice and now striving to prove his courage.

From there, Connors went to work on *Cowboy in Africa*, in which he played a rodeo champion hired to run a game ranch in Kenya. Whose idea was this, anyway? In any case, the show lasted through the 1967–1968 season and was cancelled, after which Connors took several seasons off from television. He returned in 1973 as the host of the syndicated *Thrill Seekers*, a program devoted to the presentation of death-defying feats, including cliff divers and motorcycle jumps. Like Connors's previous efforts, the show lasted one year.

Though he had a very small role in *Roots* in 1977, Connors did not make a return to series television until 1983, and then in a supporting role. The program was *The Yellow Rose*, a modern-day Texas ranching soap opera featuring

Sam Elliott, Cybill Shepherd, and David Soul (see David Soul). Connors played the show's villain, Jeb Hollister, but after one season, it was over. With the cancellation of *The Yellow Rose*, Connors had starred in five different series whose total television life added up to the run of his first series, *The Rifleman*.

Finally, in 1987, Connors found his way into a recurring role in the Fox series, *Werewolf*. Though it had a sizable cult following, the show was cancelled quickly, the sixth consecutive series starring Connors to be cancelled after one season.

Sadly, Connors would not get another crack at series television. On November 10, 1992, he died of lung cancer at age 71.

BOB CRANE

Once a popular California radio talk-show host, Crane had a small role on *The Donna Reed Show*, but first came to prominence as the wisecracking, Nazi-baffling Colonel Hogan on *Hogan's Heroes*, the much-loved CBS comedy that is still seen in reruns today. Crane played Hogan from 1965 to the show's cancellation in 1971. The basic premise of *Hogan's Heroes* was funny in itself: A group of POWs in Nazi Germany during World War II were so much smarter than their prison camp commandant and his men that they were an integral part of the resistance movement, helping fugitives escape from Germany and leaving the camp at their whim to create all manner of havoc for the opposing forces.

They had all the comforts of home, and the likable buffoon who was supposed to guard them, Sergeant Schultz, was easily persuaded to say, "I know nothing, I see nothing." Even Colonel Klink, the commandant, could be a sympathetic character at times, especially in the face of visits from SS Major Hochstetter. Sympathetic, funny Nazis? At times. Television has seen far stranger things, but the show was still a risk in the taste department. The risk paid off, though.

Hogan and his men, who included *Family Feud* host Richard Dawson, were more valuable to the war effort as POWs than as free men, though they could have walked out of the camp whenever they liked. Hogan also had an ongoing pseudoromance with Klink's secretary, Hilda.

As Hogan, Crane was the show's centerpiece. His charm and humor were natural talents and he

Bob Crane may have had his own post-*Hogan* show, but audiences just said, "I see nothing. . . ." Copyright © 1975 NBC.

brought them to their peak in the role. *Hogan's Heroes* was in the top twenty for its first two seasons, but fell off after that.

After its cancellation in 1971, Crane all but disappeared for several years before resurfacing in *The Bob Crane Show* in 1975. Crane played an insurance man who'd quit his job to go to medical school. A long way from his role as Hogan, audiences may have been uninterested in the new Crane. In any case, the show lasted only three months before being cancelled.

Sadly, Bob Crane was murdered on June 29, 1978, in Scottsdale, Arizona. According to *Newsweek*, Crane was "found beaten to death in his bedroom, with an electrical cord tied around his neck," a sobering and tragic end to the life of a man gifted with talent and humor. Mystery still surrounds the details of Crane's murder. We will never know whether Bob Crane might have made a triumphant return to television, and are the poorer for it.

PATTY DUKE

In 1962, an unknown actress named Patty Duke stunned the nation with her performance as blind deaf-mute Helen Keller, a young woman who learns to communicate through the extraordinary efforts of an amazing teacher, in *The Miracle Worker*. Duke won an Oscar for that role. It is difficult to imagine what convinced ABC that this woman, who had become famous due to her innate dramatic ability, would be a hit in a light family comedy series.

Somebody over there must have been psychic. Otherwise, *The Patty Duke Show* didn't sound like such a great idea. The star of *The Miracle Worker* would be featured as the show's *two* main characters, a gum-snapping American teenager and her bookish cousin from Scotland, who would rather play her bagpipes than listen to Bobby Vinton. Of course, it worked. The show, which based most of its humor on instances in which other cast members could not tell the two girls apart, ran for three seasons. Not a blockbuster, for sure, but enough to stay in syndicated reruns for thirty years.

Needed: One pair of matching bookends. Patty Duke with Helen Hunt and Richard Krenna in *It Takes Two*. Copyright © 1982 ABC.

Duke made several theatrical features and made-for-TV movies over the course of the next two decades, most of them forgettable. In 1979, she remade *The Miracle Worker* for television, taking the role of Helen Keller's teacher, which Anne Bancroft played in the original. She did not return to series television until 1982, when she and Richard Crenna starred in *It Takes Two*.

It Takes Two featured Crenna and Duke as a Chicago couple adjusting to a new lifestyle. He was a surgeon, and she had just abandoned years as a housewife to go to law school and become an assistant district attorney. Perhaps the best thing that can be said about this one-season turkey was that the couple's children were played by future talent Helen Hunt (*Mad About You*) and Anthony Edwards (*Northern Exposure, E.R.*).

Duke didn't wait long the next time around. When *It Takes Two* ended in 1983, she went on to play the President of the United States in *Hail to the Chief*, an ABC series by the creators of *Soap*. As goofy and unique as this show was, it lasted a mere seven episodes in the summer of 1985. Lasting only one week longer was Duke's 1987 Fox Network effort, *Karen's Song*, about a divorced woman dating a much younger man while trying to explain the whole thing to her eighteen-year-old-daughter (*Lois & Clark*'s Teri Hatcher).

Like Chuck Connors's, Duke's sophomore slump just keeps going. This Oscar-winning actress has found herself relegated to tragedy-of-the-week TV movies and awful offerings such as *Amityville 4*. Perhaps it's time to dust off

The Miracle Worker again. Either that, or a new Patty Duke show with the actress as the grandmother to a pair of look-alike cousins?

INTERLUDE

Charlie's Angels

Of the three original Angels, for it was those three who made the show a hit, two have suffered significant sophomore slumps on series television. Kate Jackson, who had earlier played the wife of one of characters in *The Rookies*, a well-known supporting role, found her first lead, and her biggest success, on *Charlie's Angels*. Her next prime time series was *Scarecrow & Mrs. King*, which lasted four seasons and was a middling success, certainly performing well enough to disqualify her as a "slump" candidate. It should be noted that her third starring role was in the series version of the film *Baby Boom* starring Diane Keaton, which lasted four months. Still, she followed up her first show with another hit, something we can't say for her two co-stars.

The story of *Charlie's Angels* was simple enough. Three women, Sabrina, Kelly, and Jill, had left the rigors of the police department to become private investigators under the auspices of Townsend Investigations. Its proprietor, Charlie Townsend (John Forsythe), was never seen, only his voice was heard, giving instructions to the "Angels" and to his second-in-command, a man named Bosley (David Doyle) who managed the firm. Jaclyn Smith played Kelly, the smart and sexy middle ground between the show's other two stars, Kate Jackson as brainy Sabrina and Farrah Fawcett-Majors as gorgeous cover girl Jill.

FARRAH FAWCETT

You've all heard the expression, "I guess you just had to be there." In the case of Farrah Fawcett-Majors and *Charlie's Angels*, those words were never so true. For many teenage American boys, *Charlie's Angels* was the first time they noticed, I mean *really* noticed, women. And how could we not? Bras were as scarce as John Forsythe's face on the show, or at least it seemed that way at the time.

Everybody had their favorite Angel. But no matter how many votes went to Smith and Jackson, America had the hots for Farrah Fawcett-Majors. (Married at the time to actor Lee Majors, she would later drop his name.) Every woman wanted to have her hair cut in that Farrah wave, every man wanted her poster, her T-shirt, her everything. Every young girl wanted the Farrah doll, and every boy wanted, very simply, to grow up fast and marry her. For one whole year, she was the female ideal in America.

And then she walked out on the show. Apparently overwhelmed and overconfident due to the spectacular celebrity she had attained in such a short time, the actress decided that she had much bigger things ahead, and left the show to try for a film career. Legal wrangling forced her to appear in several later episodes, especially to validate the introduction of Cheryl Ladd as her character's sister.

Regardless of the duration of her stay on *Charlie's Angels*, which lasted five seasons (1976–1981) and spent the first two in the top five, Farrah Fawcett-Majors had become an international star based on the success of the program. Unfortunately, the feature film career she was hoping for was not in the cards. In 1979, she made the embarrassing turkey *Sunburn*, with Charles Grodin, and in 1980 the science-fiction flop *Saturn 3* with Kirk Douglas. In 1981, she appeared in a supporting role in *Cannonball Run*, but with a cast that included Mel Tillis and Terry Bradshaw, which in itself was a huge step down.

It was not until she returned to television that Fawcett began to make people believe that she could really act and that she was not, in fact, the Jill Munroe character from *Charlie's Angels*, but rather an intelligent, mature woman with some very serious things to say. She said

Good Sports failed to score any points with the viewers, despite Farrah's obvious chemistry with Ryan O'Neal. *Copyright © 1991 ABC.*

195

them in a series of tremendously well-received television movies, for which she garnered accolades throughout the industry, and among TV audiences. The TV movies included *Murder in Texas*, *The Burning Bed*, *Between Two Women*, and the devastating *Small Sacrifices*. During this time, Fawcett also returned to features, with an acclaimed leading role in *Extremities*, as well as performances in *Double Exposure* and a little-known gem, *See You in the Morning*, which also starred Jeff Bridges, Alice Krige, and Drew Barrymore.

Fawcett had long been romantically linked with film actor Ryan O'Neal, so it was no surprise at all that when Fawcett made her television series comeback, in 1991's *Good Sports*, O'Neal would be her costar. The program concerned a hard-working cable sports network anchorwoman who must deal with the hiring of a coanchor, a less-than-intelligent former football star with whom she once had a fling. Despite the star status of the leads, *Good Sports* lasted only six months.

As a television star, Fawcett's sophomore slump, *Good Sports*, seems to have put her career on hold—she is now scarce on both large and small screens.

JACLYN SMITH

Though she would later compete with Jane Seymour for the title "Queen of the Miniseries" and enjoy a lucrative career as a pitchwoman for all manner of products, Smith's first big break was as Kelly Garrett in *Charlie's Angels*. As

196

described above, the show was one of the most successful prime time series of its era, and Kelly was its resident bad girl. When a mission called for sheer beauty, the job went to Jill, but if seduction was the name of the game, Kelly Garrett was the woman to do it.

Beautiful and soft-spoken, Smith seemed destined for her career on such TV tearjerkers as *Rage of Angels* and *Windmills of the Gods*, among many others. But after the success of *Charlie's Angels*, and keep in mind that Smith was the only original star to remain with the program for its duration, it seems surprising that it took her eight years to return to a prime time series.

In 1989, Smith finally did return to a series, sort of. Rather than a weekly half hour or hour, she returned in *Christine Cromwell*, part of the ABC Mystery Movie wheel structure, which rotated several series of two-hour movies. *Christine Cromwell* was shown once very four or five weeks, with a two-hour episode each time. While some series on the "wheel" graduated to weekly hours, or continued as series of telefilms, *Christine Cromwell* was a nonstarter,

197

Jaclyn Smith as *Christine Cromwell*. Copyright © 1989 ABC.

dead in the water. It first aired in November 1989 and had its final episode the following March, meaning a maximum of four telefilms were made with the character.

While Smith has remained a popular actress and commercial pitchwoman, she doesn't seem to be in a rush to try her hand at another prime time series, so it seems likely her slump will continue for the foreseeable future. Still, when every other aspect of a career is going as well as Jaclyn Smith's, *Christine Cromwell* has left barely a blemish.

198

REDD FOXX

Lean back, right now, put a hand over your heart, and wheeze in a raspy voice, "This is the big one, Elizabeth!" If you've ever seen the show, chances are you've imitated that quintessential Redd Foxx expression. Foxx had been a successful stand-up comedian for years before NBC gave him his own showcase on *Sanford and Son*. In fact, Foxx's material was often considered "blue," or too risque for tender television audiences. Still, NBC knew what they had when they cast the comedian as lovable old-timer Fred Sanford.

Fred eked out a living as a junkman, in partnership with his son Lamont (Demond Wilson). Lamont, however, wanted more from life, and the show's lynch pin was the threat that Lamont would one day leave Fred to run the business on his own. The relationship between father and son, and the silly cast of regular supporting characters, made *Sanford and Son* a bona fide hit. From its debut in January 1972 until it went off the air in 1977, the show was in the top ten and twice climbed as high as number two for the season.

Still going strong, *Sanford and Son* was demolished by Foxx's departure in 1977. ABC had wooed him with promises of his own variety show, and the star could not resist. The program might have revolved around Lamont Sanford after that, but Wilson wanted too much money to keep playing the character and, instead, NBC created a spin-off called *The Sanford Arms*. The spin-off program lasted only four weeks.

Foxx was luckier with his variety show, titled simply *Redd Foxx*. It lasted a whole four months before being unceremoniously yanked from the air. Whatever magic ABC thought they were stealing from their rival network, they didn't get it. Supporting characters from *Sanford and Son* made appearances from time to time, but the show relied mainly on bad old comedians who were friends of Foxx, race-based humor, and even, dare we say it, Foxx as a singer.

Eight years later, Foxx tried again with *The Redd Foxx Show*, an inner-city sitcom whose high points were the presence of Barry Van Dyke and a young comedian named Sinbad. That was 1986, and the program was off the air in three months, faster even than Foxx's previous attempt.

In 1989, Foxx had a supporting role in the film *Harlem Nights*, starring Eddie Murphy. Though the film was not a success, it did put Murphy and Foxx together and led to Murphy's producing Foxx's fourth television series. In Sep-

199

tember 1991, *The Royal Family* debuted on CBS to respectable ratings. Foxx and Della Reese, with whom he had worked a number of times, played a recently retired couple put upon by the news that their just-separated daughter and her three children were coming to live with them.

The show might have been a success, might have been the project to lift Foxx out of the sophomore slump he'd been in since his ill-advised departure from *Sanford and Son* fourteen years earlier, but it was not to be. On October 11, 1991, Redd Foxx finally had the heart attack he'd always joked about. Though his death was written into the show, and popular actress Jackee joined the cast, the clock was ticking for *The Royal Family*. In no time at all, they were off the air.

JAMES GARNER

The only significant appearance James Garner had made previous to starring in the series *Maverick* was earlier the same year, 1957, in supporting role in the film *Sayonara*, starring Marlon Brando. And then in September, he was a star. Among the most popular westerns still in syndicated reruns, *Maverick* broke the mold of traditional cowboy and gunfighter shows. The hero, here, was a less-than-brave gambler with a lot of charm, a great sense of humor, and terrible aim.

200

Garner was Bret Maverick, and actor Jack Kelly played his brother Bart. The two often took turns as the main character, or shared the story, depending on what each week called for. But Garner was always the favorite. In its second and third seasons, *Maverick* was in the top twenty, but in 1960, Garner broke his contract with Warner Brothers and left the series, demanding better terms. Though ABC brought in two new Maverick relatives, including Roger Moore as British cousin Beauregard, without Garner the show limped along for two more seasons and then was cancelled.

Garner's dispute with Warner Brothers left him free to continue with his career elsewhere, and he did just that. During the sixties, the actor appeared in a number of acclaimed films, including *The Great Escape, The Americanization of Emily, Support Your Local Sheriff, Support Your Local Gunfighter*, and *The Children's Hour*. He did not return to television until 1971, and then it was with another western.

Garner's triumphant TV return, or at least that was how it was supposed to happen, was in an early-twentieth-century western called *Nichols*. The main character returns to the town that his family had founded years earlier, and that bears his name, to find it run by a villainous matriarch. He becomes the town's sheriff, but only because the woman feels she will be able to manipulate him in that position. the show's ratings were in the basement, and at season's end, Garner's character, Nichols, was murdered, only to be avenged by his twin, also played by Garner, in an attempt to engender some viewer interest. *Nichols* had battled its way through an entire season, but Garner's TV career was bust.

That TV sophomore slump obviously affected Garner. He appeared in few films in the early seventies, and, this time, he did not stay away from television long. Two years after *Nichols* was cancelled, in the fall of 1974, the actor tried something new. As Jim Rockford in *The Rockford Files*, Garner still had the wisecracks and the grin, the charm and the fast talk, but he had a serious side TV audiences weren't used to from him. A former convict (for a crime he didn't commit, natch!), Rockford was dead serious about his job as a private detective. Audiences also loved the gimmicks Rockford used to get information and the depths he would stoop to in order to get the job done.

Though it appeared only in the top twenty-five during its first season, *The Rockford Files* was popular enough with audiences that Garner received several Emmy Awards. In 1980, Garner again walked off his own show. Of particular interest in that final 1979–1980 season was the appearance, from time to time, of a little-known actor named Tom Selleck as Rockford's competitor, private investigator Lance White. In 1983, the actor sued Universal, the show's producer, claiming that he had not received his share of syndication profits. He won $75 million.

After *The Rockford Files*, Garner didn't stay away from TV long at all.

Instead, he starred for NBC in a revival of his first star vehicle, a new show called *Bret Maverick*. Two decades after the role had made him famous, Garner was back, older now and trying to clean up the reputation of the former card hustler. Unfortunately, it seemed audiences had lost their taste for Maverick, or at least didn't need a new one. The show lasted only eight months. (The summer of 1994, however, brought Garner back into the *Maverick* mythos when he appeared in a supporting role in the new film version starring Mel Gibson and Jodie Foster.)

Garner made several memorable films in the years that followed, among them *Victor/Victoria* and *Murphy's Romance*. He returned to television again nearly a decade later, as a politician in *Man of the People*. Garner had charmed generations with a wisecrack, a grin, a con, and a scam for every character he played, and Jim Doyle was no exception. Unfortunately, the duration of his roles continued to shorten, and this 1991 effort lasted only weeks.

In recent years, Garner has received raves for his performances in such made-for-television fare as *Decoration Day* and *Barbarians at the Gate*. Though he recovered from his *Nichols* sophomore slump to make *The Rockford Files*, he is apparently in another prime time TV slump that he has yet to overcome. Interestingly, it may be *The Rockford Files* that once again puts him back on top. Recent news reports have claimed that Garner will begin making TV movies for CBS based on the old series, and who knows where that might lead.

ANDY GRIFFITH

In 1957, Andy Griffith appeared in two films, *A Face in the Crowd* and the movie that brought him to America's attention, *No Time for Sergeants*. His next major project was the leap to television, and what a leap it was, to a show named after him!

The Andy Griffith Show is widely considered to be one of the most successful prime time television series ever, and with good reason. During its eight seasons, the show never fell out of the top ten and for most of its run was within the top five. In its last season, after eight years, *The Andy Griffith Show* was number one. Its spin-offs also did well. *Gomer Pyle, U.S.M.C.*, ran for five seasons in the top ten, and of the three seasons that *Mayberry R.F.D.* lasted, it was a top ten show for two. The show launched the careers of Griffith, Don Knotts, Jim Nabors, and, of course, little Ronnie Howard, who would go on to become one of the most powerful men in Hollywood.

Add to all this that several generations of Americans can whistle the theme song to the show, and you've got real success.

But what was the formula? In Mayberry, North Carolina, a young widowed sheriff must cope with life, love, and the buffoonery of the lovable townspeople, who only mean the best for him and his young son. It was a simpler time, that's for sure, when a program with the innocence of *The Andy Griffith Show* could achieve the success that it did. But there was more to it than that. The show's timeless themes, the earnestness of its stars, and their comic abilities have given the show a thriving second life in syndication, even thirty-five years later.

For eight years, Griffith played Andy Taylor, and much of the show's warmth came through his relationship with Howard's Opie, a name for which the director-actor still receives jibes. Don Knotts was perhaps the best of the comic relief on the show, as jittery, paranoid deputy Barney Fife. Humor also came with such characters as Otis, Goober, Gomer, Howard, Aunt Bee, and, of course, Floyd the barber.

William Conrad (aka *Cannon*) makes a guest appearance on Andy Griffith's *Matlock*.

When, in its eighth season, the show had finally reached number one, Griffith had had enough, and left. With a new star in the same surroundings, the producers continued with *Mayberry R.F.D.*

Hindsight is 20/20. Griffith ought to have stayed. Instead, he returned to television in 1970's *The Headmaster*. The series, about the principal of a private school and his interactions with the staff (including the gym coach, played by none other than Jerry Van Dyke, of TV's *Coach*), was a 180 degree turn from the comedy of *The Andy Griffith Show*. It lasted four months.

Realizing that he'd made an error with *The Headmaster*, Griffith quickly put together *The New Andy Griffith Show*, which presented him as a Southern mayor. Though the show attempted to repeat the folksy comedy of the original, the magic wasn't there and the public just didn't go for it. Once again, the program lasted only four months.

That was 1971, and it would be eight years before Griffith returned to series television. He made several unremarkable films in that time, and when he did come back to TV, it was in a project equally unremarkable, a series entitled *Salvage 1*. Perhaps the only notable thing about the series, which began in January 1979 and lasted out the remainder of the season, was that it was the first in which Griffith's character was not named "Andy." Instead, he played Harry Broderick, who in hindsight was sort of Fred Sanford and MacGyver put together. Don't laugh. The character ran a salvage operation whose adventures included reclaiming satellites from space, downed airplanes from dangerous jungles, and diamonds from inside a live volcano.

Uh-huh.

In 1981 and 1983, respectively, Griffith appeared in two critically acclaimed TV movies, *Murder in Texas* and *Murder in Coweta County*. In 1985,

206

he showed up in a failed western comedy, *Rustler's Rhapsody*. Finally, in 1986, after three failed series' worth of sophomore slump, Griffith returned to television once again. This time, however, he'd picked a winner.

Matlock featured Griffith as an aging Southern gentleman-attorney, who each week became entangled in a murder mystery he would solve in his most self-effacing manner. In the top twenty for most of its run, *Matlock* eventually switched from NBC to ABC, where as of this writing it is still being aired. For Andy Griffith, the road between Andy Taylor and Ben Matlock was a long and disappointing one, but then, he who laughs last . . .

INTERLUDE

The Dukes of Hazzard

It was the ultimate teenage male hormone show. In January 1979, *The Dukes of Hazzard* debuted on CBS, starring two good ole boys, their bitchin' car, and Catherine Bach's cutoffs.

"Just'a good ole boys, never meanin' no harm. Beats all you ever saw, been in trouble with the law since the day they was born."

So sang Waylon Jennings in the theme to this long-running series. Tom Wopat and John Schneider starred as Luke and Bo Duke, respectively, two fun-

208

John Schneider and Tom Wopat never again approached the international acclaim they received with *The Dukes of Hazzard*.

loving southern boys whose favorite pastime was riling up the local mayor and sheriff. Their car, a gaudy colored Dodge Charger with the rebel flag painted on the roof, was called the "General Lee," and it was their pride and joy. Along with their Uncle Jesse (Denver Pyle) and their sexy cousin Daisy Duke (Catherine Bach), they were in and out of trouble several times each episode.

Though, due to a battle over their salaries, both Schneider and Wopat walked for a season, it was to both the show's and the stars' benefit that they came back the following year. As to the two unknowns who replaced them, they got more than their fifteen minutes and should be grateful, wherever they are.

A rip-roaring, fun-loving hour of television replete with southern hospitality and extraordinarily stupid law enforcement officials and officers, *The Dukes of Hazzard* lasted a surprising six seasons, from 1979 to 1985. Television hadn't seen a funny good ole boy since Jed Clampett, and little boys across America were wild for Dukes T-shirts, lunchboxes, thermoses . . . anything they could get their hands on. Car expos across America will still sometimes showcase the "General Lee," though there were over 300 such cars used on the program, most of them destroyed in on-camera stunts. For several years, the series was a true phenomenon.

During the first three seasons, *The Dukes of Hazzard* was a top ten show. The fourth season, which did not include Schneider and Wopat, performed miserably in the ratings. Though the stars came back the next year, it was by then too late. Viewers had gone on to something else, and the series did not appear in the top twenty-five again.

Catherine Bach, who sent male teenage hearts racing, has not starred in a TV series since, though she has appeared in several B-movies.

JOHN SCHNEIDER

If *The Dukes of Hazzard* was a funny, southern *Starsky & Hutch* (think about it!), then Schneider was clearly meant for the David Soul role. The charming blond had hearts aflutter in Hazzard County and, even more so than his co-star, became a pinup boy for the early eighties.

After the final cancellation of *The Dukes of Hazzard*, Schneider was through with television for a while. Instead, he pursued his great love, country music, and actually became fairly successful as a country singer. His TV following didn't hurt, to be sure. However, when it came time for him to return to television, four years after his hit series had been bounced off the air, he was somewhat less successful.

Okay, we're being generous. Actually, he bombed in a very big, very embarrassing way. Schneider's sophomore slump was ironically titled *Grand Slam*, and paired the actor-singer with actor-comedian Paul Rodriguez. The two played San Diego bounty hunters. Despite the action story line, which ought to have been popular with Schneider's fans, *Grand Slam* lasted a humiliating six weeks. Schneider retreated back into his music, and like Bach, has made several B-movies, but as far as primetime television is concerned, his sophomore slump continues.

TOM WOPAT

If Schneider was the eighties' Hutch, then Wopat must surely be Starsky. The black-haired, more serious Duke (if any Duke could ever be serious for more than a minute), Wopat never had Schneider's pretty boy image.

Thus it did not seem totally unlikely when he returned to prime time in the 1988 dramatic series *Blue Skies*. Following the formula of so many TV programs, Wopat played Frank Cobb, a widowed father of two who had recently married a divorced mother of one. The new family moved to Oregon where Cobb could operate the saw mill started by his father.

Like Schneider's *Grand Slam*, *Blue Skies* lasted only a dismal six weeks before being yanked from the CBS schedule. Unlike Schneider, Wopat returned for yet a third try at prime time stardom, and he wasted no time in doing it.

A year after *Blue Skies* bombed, Wopat returned in another drama, *A Peaceable Kingdom*, which co-starred *The Bionic Woman*'s Lindsay Wagner. Wopat and Wagner played a brother and sister running the Los Angeles County Zoo. Somewhat more successful than Wopat's previous effort, *A Peaceable Kingdom* lasted a whopping eight weeks on the air, before disappearing, with both its stars, from the tube.

Since that time, Wopat has been MIA.

ROBERT GUILLAUME

It's hard to forget that fall of 1977, when *Soap* debuted. The show was, to put everything else in perspective, absolutely insane. Manic and goofy, bursting the envelope, titillating the audience and making fun of all of America's sacred cows, *Soap* was pure genius and often quite stupid at the same time.

Katherine Helmond, Richard Mulligan, and Billy Crystal were particularly memorable. So, of course, was Robert Guillaume as Benson, the Butler.

The role was a beauty. In the traditionally racist role of black servant, Guillaume became instead the only sane, intelligent character in the series, aloof and clearly aware that he was superior to the rest of them. So popular was the character that he received his own series, *Benson*, in which he became the head of household for Governor Gatling.

Over the course of *Benson*'s seven seasons, he received greater and greater duties, rising from butler to state budget director to lieutenant governor, and finally running against his former boss for the governor's seat. Though the outcome of that election was never revealed, all of his fans assume that Benson won. Considering that the show was in the top twenty-five only in its first year, it is nothing short of amazing that *Benson* lasted for as long as it did. Perhaps this can be credited to Guillaume's considerable charm.

Three years passed before Guillaume's second attempt at a star vehicle. This time it was *The Robert Guillaume Show*, and the actor was playing a divorced marriage counselor whose father was upset that he was dating a white woman. Four months later, Guillaume's second effort disappeared forever into the land of bad TV shows. (Note: Only with the advent of cable channels such as Sci-Fi are some of these truly short-lived series seen again. Most programs with few episodes are never picked up for syndication, anywhere.)

The next time, he didn't wait quite as long. Only two years after the dis-

212

mal failure of *The Robert Guillaume Show*, the actor was back as a detective in a *Barney Miller*-esque comedy called *Pacific Station*, which lasted no longer than his previous effort. Guillaume has appeared in supporting roles in several films, among them *Seems Like Old Times*, *Wanted: Dead or Alive*, and *Lean on Me*.

Guillaume has yet to make another attempt at TV success, and while we wait, his slump continues.

213

LARRY HAGMAN

Based on the virtues of only two series, Hagman is one of the most successful television actors of all time. Though he's made several feature films, he has never had a lead role in a successful one. All of his celebrity stems from the tube.

Perhaps the most interesting thing about *I Dream of Jeannie* is that in the five seasons during which it was broadcast, it never finished in the top twenty-five, and yet its popularity made it one of the most widely run programs when it went to syndication. One reason for the show's consistently mediocre ratings may have been that for every season, it was shown in a different time slot.

Larry Hagman was Captain Tony Nelson, an astronaut who had been marooned on a tropical island after an aborted mission and there found an ancient bottle. Inside that bottle was a beautiful, bubble-headed genie, played by Barbara Eden. (We won't even go into the whole belly button thing, which has been recounted thousands of times.) Every man's dream, to have such a beauty call him master (at least in the sixties!). Bill Daly played Captain Roger Healey, Tony's bumbling, and very envious, best friend. During the show's final season, Jeannie and Tony were married (explain that to the neighbors).

Another show with a theme song that still sticks in the head to this day, *I Dream of Jeannie* was the most lighthearted of comedies and Hagman the most sincere straight man in ages. Even when his aw shucks persona gave way to anger, he could never stay mad at a creature as innocent as Jeannie for very long.

Hagman's next attempt at comedy came just a year after *I Dream of Jeannie* had broadcast its final episode. In 1971's *The Good Life*, Hagman and Donna Mills played a middle-class couple who are tired of their boring lives and decide to search for at least a taste of the good life by signing on to become butler and maid to a wealthy family, despite their lack of training in the proper behavior for such positions. On *Jeannie*, it had been Eden and Daly who did all the bumbling, and Hagman simply wasn't suited for it. *The Good Life* was cancelled after less than four months on the air.

Hagman's sophomore slump continued with *Here We Go Again*, which ran for five months in 1973. The title might just as well have referred to the show's chances of lasting more than a season, as audiences just didn't bother to tune into the story of newlyweds, both of whom had former spouses living nearby, and the havoc that was their life together.

It would be five years before Larry Hagman would star in another prime time series, and then he would finally end his slump. It was the role of a life-time, the one that put him forever in the firmament of American popular culture, J.R. Ewing. The show, of course, was *Dallas*.

The ultimate evening soap opera, *Dallas* featured Hagman as the eldest son of an oil-rich family and the focal point of one of the most popular TV shows of all time. As J.R., Hagman was hated by an audience around the world for his cruelty and greed. The character came to epitomize everything Americans hated about money, even more than Gordon Gecco in Oliver Stone's *Wall Street* would years later.

Surrounded by a cast of dozens, which changed constantly, Hagman was the villain's villain, but unlike other evening soap nasties, and even with all those other name actors around, he was unquestionably the star of the show. *Dallas* debuted in 1978, and by the beginning of the 1980–1981 season, in which the answer to the eternal question, "Who shot J.R.?" was finally revealed, *Dallas* would achieve a singular feat. That revelatory episode became the most watched television program in the history of the medium up to that time.

Two other episodes stand out as milestones in the long history of the series, and of television. First, after the entire previous season had dealt with the death of major character Bobby Ewing (Patrick Duffy), the 1986–1987 season premiere featured a startling revelation—not only was Bobby alive, but the whole 1985–1986 season had been one long dream, a stunt never duplicated in its sheer audacity before or since.

Second, the show's last episode, which was broadcast on May 3, 1991, presented J.R. as a broke and broken man, abandoned by everyone who had ever cared for him. A twisted riff on *It's a Wonderful Life*, the finale ended with J.R.'s apparent suicide, though the act is implied rather than presented as a certainty, leaving viewers to make their own judgment. (Where I'm from, we call that a cop-out!)

After thirteen years, seven of which *Dallas* was in the top ten, and three of which it was number one, the circus had left town. For Hagman, *Dallas* may be an impossible act to follow. But then, why should he? He's got nothing to prove.

DAVID McCALLUM

Another TV star who made a number of unsuccessful feature films, McCallum made a big splash in his first starring role, as Russian-born superspy Ilya Kuryakin, *The Man From U.N.C.L.E.* Unlike many other first shows by actors listed in this section, *The Man From U.N.C.L.E.* was far from a runaway hit. Though it ran for three and a half years, only in its second year did it even finish in the top twenty five (#13). Still, the show, which co-starred Robert Vaughn, made McCallum famous and is still popular today.

Vaughn was an American agent, Napoleon Solo, and McCallum his Russian counterpart. Together they were members of the worldwide organization, U.N.C.L.E. and spent their lives in pitched battle with the agents of the international crime organization, THRUSH. Essentially, the show was a very goofy James Bond story, its plots riddled with more holes than Swiss cheese, its villains as thin as cardboard. Still, it had a loyal following, and NBC had enough faith to spin off *The Girl From U.N.C.L.E.* in 1966. That lasted one season.

When the show was cancelled in 1968, McCallum began a seven-year absence from series television. That ended in the fall of 1975, when he appeared in his second TV series,

217

Once an Ilya, always an Ilya. David McCallum (r.) with Robert Vaughn (l), and Leo G. Carroll (center), the men from *U.N.C.L.E.*

another fantasy story line no more plausible than *The Man From U.N.C.L.E.*'s. In his new show, McCallum played doctor Daniel Westin, *The Invisible Man*. This series turned the character into a sort of superhero by providing him with a wig, lifelike mask, and hand-gloves that allowed him to continue with his life while performing dangerous investigations on the side with his wife.

Forever remembered as Ilya Kuryakin, McCallum's sophomore slump began and ended with *The Invisible Man*, which lasted four months.

He never returned to series television.

INTERLUDE

Three's Company

Based on the British series, *Man About the House*, *Three's Company* was America's guilty pleasure for seven and a half seasons (the half being the show's trial run in spring 1977). The show featured Joyce DeWitt and Suzanne Somers as a couple of California girls in need of a third roommate to make the rent on their new apartment. They find one in Jack Tripper (John Ritter), who is able to move in despite the complaints of their landlords, the Ropers, only because he claims to be gay.

The show relied greatly on showing DeWitt and Somers in their sleep-wear, on the sexual innuendoes they traded with Ritter and Richard Kline as Jack's friend, Larry, and Mr. Roper's (Norman Fell) constant jokes about Jack's alleged sexual preference. Roper seemed to genuinely like Jack, but it got under his skin that his new tenant supposedly liked other men.

Three's Company was in the top ten, and frequently the top five, through-out its run, with the exception of its initial half season, when it was number eleven, and its final season, when it didn't make the top twenty-five at all. By the third season, *The Ropers* had spun off into their own show, which lasted one year. They were replaced as landlord by classic funnyman Don Knotts, a welcome addition to the cast.

Only two of the three main performers in this series truly belong in this book. Like Elizabeth Montgomery of *Bewitched*, and Bonnie Franklin and Mackenzie Phillips of *One Day at a Time*, Joyce DeWitt, who played Janet, has never returned to series television and therefore has no sophomore effort to cri-tique. Her costars, on the other hand . . . oh, boy.

JOHN RITTER

Though John Ritter had spent four seasons as Reverend Fordwick on *The Wal-tons*, he left the series for his first starring role, as Jack Tripper in *Three's Company*. His comic timing was one of the things that kept the show at the top for

John Ritter with Felton Perry (left) in *Hooperman*, a post–*Three's Company* dud. *Copyright © 1987 Twentieth Century Fox Film Corporation. All rights reserved.*

220

the duration of its run and has kept him in the spotlight ever since, though his sophomore slump arguably (we'll explain momentarily) continues to this day.

After *Three's Company* met its final fate in 1984, Ritter kept the character of Jack Tripper alive in *Three's a Crowd*, more a sequel than a spin-off. The character had met, fallen in love, and moved in with a woman. Her father, anxious and angry, bought the building in which the couple lived, and in which Tripper had his restaurant. The series lasted one season.

John Ritter next starred in *Hooperman*, an odd variety of television series combining comedy and drama. The main character was a sensitive San Francisco police detective who also owned his apartment building and had to deal with his tenants, his insecure boss, and a roller coaster affair with his building's handyman, Susan (Deborah Farentino). Like other programs that attempted to combine the two genres,

Hooperman died, but was more fortunate than some in that it limped through two whole seasons on ABC.

Ritter's fourth starring role in a network series was in *Hearts Afire*. He played the chief aid to an Arkansas Senator, living in Washington, D.C., and Markie Post was the Senator's new scriptwriter. The two ostensibly hated each other, but their primal sexual attraction drew them together anyway (or so we're asked to believe). Eventually they would get married. While *Hearts Afire* is still on the air as of this writing, it has been on hiatus twice, and the setting has moved back to Arkansas. Having finished in seventy-eight position in the 1993–1994 TV season, its chances for survival are not promising. Ritter's slump continues.

John Ritter has made many films, but only some were at all successful. Those included *Skin Deep* and the pair of hit *Problem Child* films.

SUZANNE SOMERS

Playing the ditzy but sexy Chrissy Snow on *Three's Company* made Somers perhaps the most recognizable member of the cast. This notoriety led to Somers's falling into that age-old trap . . . believing her own press. To continue with the show, she demanded an inordinate sum of money, which producers declined to provide. There is no doubt that her decision to leave the series in 1981 was unwise, as her career plummeted thereafter.

Suzanne Somers and the cast of *She's the Sheriff*.

222

Her few feature film appearances nothing to speak of, Somers basically disappeared for six years until popping up in a prime time syndicated show called *She's the Sheriff* in 1987, six years after departing *Three's Company*. In the series, Somers portrayed a woman who takes over her late husband's job as sheriff of a small town, much to the dismay of the deputy who'd been in line for a promotion. A flatter comedy is difficult to imagine, and it is likely that only due to the nature of syndication did the show make it through two seasons.

Finally, in 1991, Somers broke her slump by appearing with *Dallas* star Patrick Duffy in the *Brady Bunch* rip-off, *Step by Step*. While it would be hard to imagine a stranger pair based on their previous efforts, audiences enjoyed the series enough to keep it on the air for three seasons as of this writing. The program finished the season at number thirty-eight and therefore seems in no imminent danger. So Somers is one step ahead of former costar John Ritter.

Not to mention that whole "Thighmaster" thing, which we won't even go into.

JIM NABORS

It's testament to the longevity of *The Andy Griffith Show* that most readers will find it difficult to imagine that Jim Nabors did not appear as Gomer Pyle on the program until its fourth season. And testament to Nabors's performance is the fact that most will find it hard to believe he stayed only for that year. The character was a happy, sincere, almost childlike fellow who pumped gas for a living. America loved him, the network loved him, and so, of course, he got his own series.

Gomer Pyle, U.S.M.C. featured Pyle quitting his job as a Mayberry gas man to join the Marine Corps—in peacetime no less. Gomer's stint with the Marines was unusual to say the least. He spent the late sixties in the corps without ever going to Vietnam! Stationed at Camp Henderson, California, Private Pyle was forced to deal with a rough, tough Corps Sergeant named Vince

Carter (Frank Sutton). Sergeant Carter was forever flummoxed by Pyle's naivete, but was eventually won over. The show also featured recurring roles for two other familiar prime time faces: Larry Hovis, who appeared for one season before moving on to play a character named, coincidentally, Carter on *Hogan's Heroes*, and William Christopher, who was with the show throughout and later played Father Mulcahy on *M*A*S*H*.

(Sorry to interrupt this book, but have you ever wondered why we say an actor was "in" a movie, and "on" a television show? Just curious.)

Over the course of its five seasons, *Gomer Pyle, U.S.M.C.* finished in the top ten every year, and for its first two years, beat *The Andy Griffith Show* from which it had spun off. While still in the top ten, *Gomer Pyle* ended so that Nabors could go on to *The Jim Nabors Hour*, a variety program that showcased the actor's other talent, singing. He had quite a bit of success with his musical career, but the program did not fare as well. Though not nearly on the level of many other slumps in this section—it lasted through two seasons of television—*the Jim Nabors Hour* finished thirteenth in its first year, disappeared from the rankings in its second, and then it was gone for good.

TONY RANDALL

Randall has appeared in numerous films, including 1951's *The Mating Game* with Debbie Reynolds, *Pillow Talk* with Rock Hudson and Doris Day, Woody

Allen's *Everything You Always Wanted to Know About Sex (But Were Afraid to Ask)*, and the wonderfully weird *7 Faces of Dr. Lao* (which Michael Jackson has recently announced his intention to remake). Despite this, however, he has and always will be known primarily as a television actor, and in that medium, as Felix Unger, of *The Odd Couple*.

Randall's TV career began far earlier, however. In the fifties he had supporting roles in *One Man's Family* and *Mr. Peepers*. No matter, it was the uptight, hypochondriac, paranoid persona of Felix Unger that would be Randall's first starring TV role. It would make him truly famous, even though Jack

From Unger: A scene from *The Tony Randall Show*.

Lemmon had originated the role in the film of the same name, which in turn had been based on Neil Simon's play. Randall is the Felix America remembers,

225

with the whining, sniffling, and just plain decency that drove Jack Klugman's Oscar Madison crazy.

And what an odd couple they were, Felix and Oscar. The two recently divorced men shared an apartment but were constantly driving one another bonkers because Felix was the ultimate neat-freak, constantly cleaning and complaining, while sports reporter Oscar was a total and complete slob. Their attempts to reunite with their ex-wives, between girlfriends of course, and the awkward presence of Felix at Oscar's poker games made for wonderful comedy.

What raised the series to the level of greatness, however, was a combination of two things: talented actors and excellent scripts. Randall and Klugman were prefect for the roles and phenomenally gifted individuals. The writing on the series showed clearly that though the two men couldn't stand one another (especially Oscar toward Felix), each genuinely cared for the other's well-being. Like siblings who are constantly at one another's throats, and yet fight off the local bullies for their brother or sister, the odd couple looked out for one another.

Beginning in 1970 and running for five successful seasons, *The Odd Couple* always managed to fall somewhat short of the top twenty-five. Still, it was very popular, and audiences still tune in regularly to syndicated repeats. In 1982 ABC attempted to resurrect the concept with *The New Odd Couple*, this time with an all-black cast including *Barney Miller*'s Ron Glass. The show flopped miserably.

The year after *The Odd Couple* was cancelled, Randall returned with *The Tony Randall Show*. Though it ran for a season and a half, from the fall of 1976 until the spring of 1978, the show performed quite poorly and certainly did not achieve the popularity of the actor's previous series. In *The Tony Randall Show*, he portrayed Philadelphia-based Judge Walter Franklin, a stuffy middle-aged man trying to get back into some semblance of a social life two years after his wife has passed away. It wasn't that long before the show passed away.

Randall's third starring role in a TV series was enigmatic. The 1981 pilot movie, called *Sidney Shorr*, had portrayed the title character as gay. When the series, retitled *Love, Sidney*, hit the airwaves, the homosexual aspects of the story were vaguely implied, but nothing more. Sidney had befriended a young actress (Swoosie Kurtz) and her daughter, who moved in with him. The series revolved around their relationship. Though *Love, Sidney* survived on NBC for two years, it spent the first quarter of 1983 on hiatus. It limped along with enough interest to inspire NBC to give it a reprieve, but never pulled in enough viewers to be considered even a marginal success.

Randall never returned to series television. Instead, he has dedicated himself to the National Actors' Theatre, a benefit organization that he helped to found, and with which he and Klugman travel the country performing Neil Simon's original theatrical version of *The Odd Couple*. As long as Felix and Oscar are out there bickering, the rest of us may sleep comfortably at night.

ADAM WEST

West had spent one season on the cop show *The Detectives, Starring Robert Taylor* (1961–1962) before making it big in the role that changed his life. Though it ran barely two seasons, *Batman* was a huge hit, surviving to the present day in syndication and foremost in the memories of the generations who watched it. So overwhelming was this campy, goofy series, that when the 1989 film *Batman* was released, with the dark creations of director Tim Burton, many audience members had a hard time taking it seriously. In fact, there was a rather large group of diehard fans who wished to see Cesar Romero as the Joker, and Adam West as Batman, including, according to reports, West himself.

Stemming from the 1939 comic book creation of artist Bob Kane and writer Bill Finger, *Batman* was originally a creature of the night, a caped superhero whose presence spread fear throughout the criminal community. In the ABC TV series, the whole thing was played for laughs. West's corny, preachy delivery, his soft middle, Robin's (Burt Ward) wide-eyed ignorance, the constant guest stars—it was all in good fun. Interestingly, the actors portraying the villains, such as the Penguin (Burgess Meredith), Egghead (Vincent Price), the Riddler (Frank Gorshin), the Joker (Romero), and Catwoman (Eartha Kitt, Lee Meriwether, or Julie Newmar, depending on the episode), seemed to have as much fun, but were still able to come off as gleefully evil.

Perhaps the show's biggest joke was the superimposition of "sound

228

effects" during the program's fight scenes. "Biff, pow, bam ... " You get the picture. The narration was also a hoot, with its constant references to "millionaire Bruce Wayne" and "stately Wayne manor." In its first season, *Batman* aired twice a week! Wednesday episodes would end with a cliff-hanger, which would be resolved on Thursday. That year, both nights of the series appeared separately in the top ten.

By the following year, despite the addition of Yvonne Craig as Batgirl, the hottest phenomenon on television had already begun to cool, cut back to once a week. By the middle of March, *Batman*-fever, and the series, had run its course, and the program did not make the top twenty-five, despite its incredible success the previous year.

It would be almost two decades before Adam West returned to a prime time series. In 1986, he starred in the sitcom *The Last Precinct*, as police Captain Rick Wright. The show concerned a precinct full of misfits, led by West, which included many unfortunate stereotypes as part of its humor. Ernie Hudson (*Ghostbusters*) was one of West's co-stars. Six weeks into its run, *The Last Precinct* met a merciful fate. West will always be remembered as *Batman*, but

Batman's Adam West as Captain Rick Wright in the sitcom *The Last Precinct*. Copyright © 1985 NBC.

he has humor and charm that could pull him out of this sophomore slump should he ever get the opportunity.

HENRY WINKLER

"Aaaaaayyyyy!"

Long before Siskel & Ebert claimed "two thumbs up" as their own, Winkler had made the gesture, along with the sighing syllable above, his trademark. In January 1974, *Happy Days* debuted on ABC, with Winkler as fifth banana, Arthur "Fonzie" Fonzarelli. In no time at all it was clear that the most popular thing about the show was the leather-clad, motorcycle-riding, high school dropout, philosopher-mechanic played by Winkler. All the girls loved him and would crowd around at the snap of a finger, and all the guys desperately wanted to be like him.

Winkler quickly moved up in the credits to just after star Ron Howard, and then to first upon Howard's 1980 departure. To show just how clearly Fonzie was the star of the show, one need look no further than the paraphernalia issue with his likeness at the time. Lunchboxes, T-shirts, posters . . . not many had Richie or Ralph Malph on them. No, it was Fonz all the way.

Winkler's first big movie role, as Butchie in *The Lords of Flatbush* (1974), was not that far a cry from his TV character, except that Butchie was not nearly as cool. During his tenure on *Happy Days*, Winkler starred in three other films—the Vietnam-themed *Heroes*, with Sally field and Harrison Ford; the college wrestling film *The One and Only*; and he hilarious Ron Howard–directed comedy *Night Shift*, with Michael Keaton and Shelley Long.

It didn't matter. *Happy Days* ran for a decade, and for all of those Americans who grew up on the show, Winkler would always be the Fonz. The charisma, humor, and sensitivity with which he imbued the character was clearly his own. In fact, it would not be too much of a stretch to say that Henry Winkler is the reason *Happy Days* lasted for ten years. Of its eleven seasons, *Happy Days* spent eight in the top twenty-five, three in the top five, and one at number one. Four series, *Laverne & Shirley*, *Mork & Mindy*, *Joanie Loves Chachi*, and *Out of the Blue* spun off from *Happy Days*. In fact, for the 1977–1978 season, *Happy Days*, *Laverne & Shirley*, and *Mork & Mindy* made up three of the top four shows.

Winkler was done with acting for a time and instead turned his efforts to producing and directing. From 1985 to 1991, he produced the popular science-adventure series *MacGyver*. He also produced tow less successful series, 1983's *Ryan's Four* and 1986's *Mr. Sunshine*. He has directed several feature films, including the 1988 Billy Crystal starrer, *Memories of Me*, and the Burt Reynolds flop, *Cop and a Half*.

During the 1993–1994 TV season, Henry Winkler finally returned to primetime television, starring in the Fox sitcom, *Monty*. Well-known for his liberal views, Winkler's being cast as a Rush Limbaugh–type talk show host may have been a stretch both for performer and for audience. In any case, the show performed dismally, finishing 119 out of 128 in the seasonal ranking, ahead of only two non-Fox programs. Needless to say, *Monty* was cancelled fairly expediently.

Nevertheless, it seems likely that Winkler will continue to be a presence in American entertainment, whether in front of or behind the cameras, for the foreseeable future. One would hope, however, that when he returns once again to acting in prime time, he finds a vehicle more worthy of his warmth and intelligence.

✳ ✳ ✳

PART FIVE: AUTHORS

How can you write a book called *Sophomore Slumps* and not mention the books that suffered from this syndrome? How indeed.

While many think that the publishing business has become just another arm of the general "entertainment industry," the art of publishing, selling, and reading books remains stubbornly peculiar enterprise. Tens of thousands of new volumes appear every year, competing for readers' attention with movies, TV, video games, software, sleep, and going to work, to mention just a few activities. Yet in that onslaught of titles, a certain number of books and authors stand out as clearly identifiable stars, bankable names that publishers pay big bucks to keep in their stables, such as Stephen King, Anne Rice, Judith Krantz, et al. And this is not a recent phenomenon. Look at back issues of magazines from the sixties or seventies and it's hard to find a best-seller list without a title by James Michener, William Manchester, Sidney Sheldon, or Jackie Suzanne.

Once established as heavyweights, it's difficult, if not impossible, for such writers *not* to hit the list. Julia Roberts and Arnold Schwarzenegger may have an occasional dog, but Stephen King, Tom Clancy, and John Grisham keep churning out hits. In fact, publishing is unique in its ability to take obscure, previously released books and turn them into best-sellers. John Grisham's *A Time to Kill* had languished unread until Doubleday had a blockbuster with his sophomore effort, *The Firm*. Eager to fan the flames of Grishamania, the clever folks at Doubleday dusted off *A Time to Kill* and soon had another money-maker on their hands. This retrospective art of marketing is peculiar to publishing. After all, all the *Rocky*s in the world have not turned *Rebel* into a box office success.

In an industry where success and name-recognition almost guarantee continued sales, true sophomore slumps are few and far between. For that reason, this section is the shortest in the book and focuses on those writers whose follow-up efforts to their breakthrough works were perceived as bona fide letdowns. These slumps may not be second efforts but books that appeared in the wake of their initial fame.

WILLIAM PETER BLATTY

The work that changed William Peter Blatty's life, the novel that skyrocketed him to international celebrity, was not the beginning of greater things for the author but, rather, the peak of his career. Blatty had started out as a humorist,

234

with his novel *Which Way to Mecca, Jack?* A quick shot on the *Jack Paar Show* to promote the book impressed the wife of a Columbia Pictures executive, and in no time Blatty was a successful comedy screenwriter. Perhaps his most famous early comedy script was Blake Edwards's *A Shot in the Dark*, the first "Pink Panther" film.

During that time, he wrote several novels with middling success. But in 1969, his screenwriting work seemed to have disappeared, so he threw himself completely into an idea that had been percolating in his brain for quite some time. In 1971, *The Exorcist* hit the stands. Based on actual events, the story of a young girl possessed by a demon became a national best-seller and, with a screenplay by the author, was transformed into one of the most talked about, controversial films ever made.

The Exorcist was the first blatantly horrific novel to reach number one on the lists, and it did so with gusto, staying there for twelve weeks. While *Time* predicted its success, the magazine also blasted Blatty's "superficial theology" and said his novel was "pretentious, tasteless and abominably written." On the other hand, other periodicals, including *Newsweek*, *Life*, the *Boston Globe*, the *New York Times Book Review*, *Los Angeles Magazine*, and *Publishers Weekly*, were effusive in their praise of the book.

While his editor, publisher, and fans all urged Blatty to write another horror novel right away, preferably a sequel to *The Exorcist*, he resisted their influence. Perhaps the most adamant were book retailers, who were consequently also the most vocal in their complaints when, instead, he wrote a book called *I'll Tell Them I Remember You*, a nonfiction reminiscence about his mother. Today, though some of Blatty's pre-*Exorcist* books are still remembered, hardly anyone has even heard of the one that followed it.

The author had nothing to do with the film sequel, *Exorcist II: The Heretic*, which is discussed in disdainful detail elsewhere in this book. One interesting anecdote, however, concerns the efforts of one of the sequel's creators to novelize it. So repulsed was he by the screenplay alone, Blatty turned down $100,000 he'd been offered to allow that book to be published.

If one does not consider *I'll Tell Them I Remember You* to be Blatty's next work—he was known for fiction, not nonfiction—his sophomore slump existed nonetheless due to a psychological suspense novel called *The Ninth Configuration*. A reworking of his earlier novel, *Twinkle, Twinkle, Killer Kane*, the book attracted a mere fraction of the audience that Blatty ought to have expected to carry over from *The Exorcist*, despite the fact that he wrote, produced, and directed a film version.

In 1983, twelve years after the publication of *The Exorcist*, Blatty finally did published a sequel, *Legion*. The book sold respectably well but, despite its relationship to the first, did not come near its success. Controversy erupted when the author attempted to sue the *New York Times* for allegedly tinkering with data to create the list as they desired.

Blatty tried for years to have the sequel made into a film and finally succeeded in 1990. Written and directed by the author, *Exorcist III: Legion* did mediocre business, performed well on video, and didn't get the attention it deserved for great performances by George C. Scott and the inimitable Brad Dourif (who later played a suspiciously similar character on an episode of TV's *The X-Files*).

More than a decade after *Legion*, Blatty has yet to publish another novel, and only *The Exorcist* remains in print.

237

INTERLUDE

The Rise and Continued Fall of the Literary Brat Pack

Though their sales never equaled the sheer numbers of those of King, Grisham, Krantz, or Clancy, for many, the literary trio of Jay McInerney, Bret Easton Ellis, and Tama Janowitz symbolized everything readers either loved or hated about the 1980s. McInerney's *Bright Lights, Big City*, Ellis's *Less than Zero*, and Janowitz's breakthrough second effort, *Slaves of New York*, were such a big sensation by mid-decade that it seemed only a matter of months before critics and disgruntled fellow novelists were sharpening their knives to skewer their follow-up efforts. What followed was a collective meltdown of the literary careers of three writers who may have received too much good ink too soon and were perceived as justifiably getting their due. *Spy* magazine, another publishing institution associated with the heady days of Reagan, *Remington Steele*, and rampant cocaine abuse, even lampooned the three writers together in a parody of *Cliff Notes* for those yuppies too busy to read the real thing.

JAY McINERNEY

Ever since F. Scott Fitzgerald called his the "lost generation," readers have looked to novelists to speak for them and summarize the angst, ennui, and drinking styles of their particular eras. Fast forward to 1984, the year of Ronald Reagan's "Morning in America" landslide over Mondale and Ferraro, America's cakewalk at the Los Angeles Olympics, and Michael Jackson's moonwalk. Filled with knowing references to a very *New Yorker*-type magazine, all-night parties, "Bolivian marching powder," models, Talking Heads lyrics, sex, and self-pity, *Bright Lights, Big City* was written in a clever, engaging second-person ("You do this, you do that") style that hooked thousands of young readers who had never before had the experience of someone writing about how *they* lived. Maybe McInerney *was* the novelist of his generation. At least some critics thought so. Writing in the *New Republic*, Terrance Moran called *BLBC* "an accomplished and funny novel full of clever verbal contraptions and hip social pastiches."

Before arriving at what seemed to be overnight success, McInerney had spent some time at the Syracuse Writing program, studying and apparently befriending (short story stylist) Raymond Carver, an inspiration to a generation of writers, who employed his penchant for everyday language and everyday people in everyday places to create a writing style often described as "K mart fiction." Though he has since died, in 1993 Carver's stories were the basis for Robert Altman's *Short Cuts*, a sprawling three and a half hour saga of contemporary L.A.

Bright Lights was remarkable for the fact that it was released directly into trade paperback without ever appearing in hardcover. McInerney's publisher, Vintage, felt that young readers, clearly Jay's audience, did not buy hardcovers. The gamble paid off, and McInerney became a publishing phenomenon.

Flushed with success and all that it brings, McInerney obliged his growing army of critics and ill-wishers by leading a public life every bit as besotted as that of the book's protagonists. His constant appearance at the right clubs, parties,

Kiefer Sutherland and Michael J. Fox in the failed film version of *Bright Lights, Big City*.

and gossip columns quickly wore out his welcome as the writer of the moment. When he took up with Marla Hanson, a model who gained celebrity when her face was horribly slashed by a psycho-photographer, snickers could be heard from coast to coast. The voice of his generation was quickly becoming a self-parody, a tabloid publicity hound.

The reception to *Ransom*, his follow-up book, was chilling. Critics panned it and readers didn't buy it. Based on McInerney's student days in Japan, *Ransom* didn't strike as many familiar chords with readers anxious to peruse another ode to the Odeon bar. Writing in the *New Republic*, Ron Lowenshon was unkind: "[Ransom] rarely rises above the level of mere competence. . . . [He is] thoroughly conventional, thoroughly uninspired. . . . The book reads like an uncertain first novel."

McInerney's subsequent efforts brought him no closer to *Bright Lights'* sales or success. The eighties turned to the nineties and his books continued to get panned. The *New York Times Book Review* called *The Story of My Life* a "pallid version of *Bright Lights*" and said the book "read like the random jottings of a zonked out teenager." *Brightness Falls* was touted as an insider's guide to publishing and the whole writing biz, but it was no bigger a hit with the critics or bookbuyers. Malcolm Jones slam dunked it in *Newsweek*: "an overstuffed novel that collapses under its own melodramatic weight."

To this day, McInerney still shows up at the right parties and gets quoted in glossy magazines and on the *New York Posts*'s "Page Six," but he yet suffers from the curse of any writer who has become a celebrity: He is more read about than read.

BRETT EASTON ELLIS

Hot on the heels of *Bright Lights*, publishers all over New York scrambled for the Next Big Thing. *Less Than Zero* more than fit the bill. Not only was it a tale of drugs, ennui, dissipation, bisexuality, and stylish dreariness among the children of L.A.'s beautiful movers and shakers, it was written by a kid *still in college*! Unlike the kids in *St. Elmo's Fire*, Brett Ellis hadn't even waited for his BA to lose his bearings. The book, a very slim hardcover with its title taken from an Elvis Costello song, was an immediate must-read in the summer and fall of 1985.

Years younger than McInerney, Ellis was not the voice of *his* generation. *Film Comment* proclaimed that the "MTV Novel Has Arrived," and *Rolling Stone* chronicled the undergraduate's life in a story entitled "Down and Out at Bennington College."

Ellis's bad boy reputation being half of the charm of his publicity tour, he more than obliged his fans with all of the necessary antics and outrages befitting a tortured young writer. In 1994, he admitted to having several post-

241

Zero nervous breakdowns before he even graduated from Bennington College, a tiny, very expensive school in Vermont, very far from the poolside binges described in *Less Than Zero*.

Two years into his reputation, Ellis penned *The Rules of Attraction* and nobody seemed to care. Less flamboyant in his fabulousness than McInerney, Ellis might have fallen into obscurity had he not written his third book, *American Psycho*. The tale of Pat Bateman, a label-obsessed stockbroker-serial killer, *Psycho* was the most notorious novel of 1990 and in many ways symbolized the popular culture's turn in taste from the get-and-spend eighties to the nineties climate of political correctness.

Just before Ellis's publisher, Simon and Schuster, was scheduled to release the book, both *Spy* and *Time* magazines published particularly gruesome passages revealing Bateman's rather clinical obsession with dismembering women. Appalled by what he read, Simon and Schuster publisher Dick Snyder yanked the book at the very last minute, let him keep his $300,000 advance, and sent him packing. Many in the gossip-prone publishing business thought Snyder had acted in an unprofessional manner. After all, he had had plenty of chances to review the manuscript before. It didn't seem right to edit or abort publications based on what he read in *Spy*. Ellis's editor was said to have been publicly humiliated by Snyder's snit. Soon the whole *Psycho* affair escalated from the publishing columns to the business pages, where rumors were flying that S&S was in serious disarray. There were reports that Martin Davis, CEO of Paramount, Simon and Schuster's parent corporation, had put the kibosh on *Psycho*. (We'll have no violence here—we're a movie company!) Sonny Mehta of Random House quickly scooped up *Psycho* and published it. Some said he did it to defend free speech and authors' rights; others saw a quick way to pour salt in Snyder's wounds and diss a crosstown rival. Controversy being the best form of publicity, *Psycho* soon found itself on the best-seller list despite howls of protest from people who found it obscene and critics who found it absurd. Writing on the *Psycho*-drama in the *New York Times*, Roger Rosenblatt observed, "*American Psycho* is the sort of journal Dorian Grey would have written if he were a high school sophomore. But that's unfair to sophomores."

Ellis' fourth book, *The Informers*, met with a cool, sometimes hostile reception upon its 1994 release. *Entertainment Weekly*, for instance, gave the book an 'F'.

243

Less Than Zero's murky, moody atmosphere did not translate to the screen. Robert Downey Jr. (left) and Andrew McCarthy (right).

TAMA JANOWITZ

Bursting on the scene with her second book, *Slaves of New York*, in 1986, Janowitz quickly assumed the mantle of the witty, wordy woman who makes devastatingly clever observations about the way we live now. (Or at least the way people who include themselves in the small incestuous world of New York's striving artists, writers, creators, poseurs live now.) If McInerney was the Fitzgerald of the moment, Janowitz was the Brady generation's answer to Dorothy Parker, or at least an update of Fran Leibowitz, the *Interview* columnist who had sent tongues wagging in the 1970s with her witty, never-to-be-followed-up debut, *Metropolitan Diary*. It's difficult to pinpoint just when Janowitz became part of the Brat Pack firmament along with Jay and Brett, but a good place to start may be Jay McInerney's 1986 rave for *Slaves of New York* in the *New York Times Book Review*, where he rhapsodized about her "shrewd observations and skewed inventions" and her "gift of singular talent."

Like her fellow Brat-Packers, she quickly became a symbol of the literary life as party-scene, where writing and thinking took a back seat to schmoozing and drinking. As you can imagine by now, the critics were ready with their brass knuckles when *A Cannibal in Manhattan* appeared in 1987. Writing in the *New Republic*, Louis Menard observed that "the novel is such a desultory affair that if I gave it a plot summary I might be accused of overanalyzing." Terrence Rafferty, who has since succeeded Pauline Kael as the chief film critic at the

New Yorker, used that magazine as a forum to skewer Janowitz, Ellis, and their whole generation: "[Ellis] and Janowitz never promised us great novels so we won't judge them by that standard. Their novels promise nothing and they are good as their word. But even if we resist the impulse to charge these young writers with the end of literature as we know it, it's depressing to read them and impossible not to feel a little nostalgic for earlier generations' grandiose ideas about the novel and for the earnest dogged craft with which the postwar novelists tried to live up to them." *Whew*!

While her post-*Slave* efforts have not been well received, Janowitz remains a recognizable literary figure. So recognizable that she has appeared in several print advertisements as the "kooky" half of an unlikely tandem. In one liquor ad she appears, standing on a piano, next to noted historian and former presidential advisor Arthur Schlesinger Jr. (Let's hope Schlesinger got a lot of money for *that*!) In a more recent outing, Janowitz is teamed up with a rather frumpy woman

Wearing an ashtray tam-o-shanter did not make Bernadette Peters funny or believable in *Slaves of New York* Copyright © 1989 Tri-Star Pictures, Inc. All rights reserved.

245

as they both reveal the secrets of what they keep on the hard-drives of their Apple Powerbook computers.

You've Read the Books, Now Rent the Movies

Like many hot books of the moment, *Bright Lights*, *Less Than Zero*, and *Slaves of New York* were all made into movies. And like other hot books, *Valley of the Dolls*, *The Carpetbaggers*, *The Other Side of Midnight*, to mention but a few, they all bombed when translated to celluloid. All three films included some remarkable talent, but never captured the magic of the written word. Filled with dark, almost poetic passages and very little action, *Less Than Zero* should have seemed almost impossible to film. Instead, it was almost impossible to watch, despite the efforts of then-hot Jami Gertz and Andrew McCarthy, as well as Robert Downey Jr., who has gone on to better films.

Slaves was produced by the incredibly toney Merchant-Ivory team whose *Room With a View* and *Howards End* have brought much joy to the *Masterpiece Theater* crowd. Perhaps their approach was not appropriate for a tale of the East Village art scene. Then again, the acting of Bernadette Peters, a forty-something chanteuse as a twenty-something heroine, might have something to do with it. The book was funny; the film was laughable.

Bright Lights, Big City consumed the efforts of a stellar cast on its way to box office flopdom. Imagine the films you could make with talent like Kiefer

Sutherland, Phoebe Cates, Swoosie Kurtz, John Houseman, and Dianne Wiest. Again, the lead role may have contributed more than its share to the film's failure. Michael J. Fox has been trying to shed is *Family Ties/Back to the Future* clean-cut-kid-next-door image for the better part of the last decade. Film audiences had a better time believing in him as *Doc Hollywood* than as a troubled fact-checker for a literary magazine. Try as they might, both Michael J. Fox and Jay McInerney may seem too much like relics of the eighties for their own good.

If it's any consolation to Jay, Brett, and Tama, *Spy* hasn't had such an easy time in the nineties either.

MARIO PUZO

Nearly every person who has ever heard of Mario Puzo knows him for one book, *The Godfather*. It matters little that Puzo is the author of four other novels, or that he is a well-respected screenwriter whose work includes the number one movie of 1979, *Superman* (no joke!). No, Puzo will always be "the man who wrote *The Godfather*."

There are worse fates.

Puzo is far from prolific. In 1955, he received $3,500 for his first novel, *The Dark Arena*, and his second novel did not appear until a decade later, when he was paid $3,000 for *The Fortunate Pilgrim*. Both books were generally well reviewed, but sold miniscule numbers (pre-*Godfather*, of course). Then a strange thing happened. Somebody suggested that Puzo could make some serious money writing a book about the Mafia. Based on a ten-page outline, Putnam paid him $5,000 in advance for the hardcover rights.

And the paperback rights sold for $410,000. While Puzo did not believe that *The Godfather* was his best work, he had obviously done something right. The story of a young Sicilian-American's reluctant rise to power in America's underworld still captivates audiences decades later, and the trilogy of films made by Francis Ford Coppola remain among the most popular dramas in history.

The *Godfather* spent a total of sixty-seven weeks on the *New York Times* best-seller list, including five months at number one. It has been published around the world in dozens of languages. Half a million hardcover copies had been sold as of 1989, and more than ten million copies in paperback. The film version of *The Godfather* won three Oscars, for Best Picture, Best Actor (Marlon Brando), and Best Screenplay, an honor shared by Puzo and cowriter Coppola.

Within the mind of Mario Puzo was born one of the greatest American stories ever told. That should be enough for the author, because his subsequent novels have not even approached the success or impact of *The Godfather*. All of those books—*The Sicilian*, which was made into a truly awful film by *Heaven's Gate* director Michael Cimino; *The Fourth K*, one of the many books of late to appear in the new sub-genre I delightedly call "Kennedy fantasy"; and *Fools*

Die—garnered serviceable reviews and sold well enough, for the most part, to make the best-seller lists. Even so, none can be considered more than a mediocre hit in comparison with *The Godfather*.

Perhaps it is unfair to Puzo to say that *The Godfather* was by far the peak of his career as a writer. And yet, almost anything would pale by comparison with the success of that book; a sophomore slump in his case was almost inevitable. Or at least it seems so in hindsight. However, even had his later novels not been less successful than their predecessor, Puzo would have a hallowed place in this book.

Though *Fools Die* was Puzo's first novel after huge hit, it was not his next book. No, like William Peter Blatty's, Puzo's next book was nonfiction. Also like Blatty's, that book faded into oblivion almost as quickly as it appeared. Puzo's follow-up was *Inside Las Vegas*, a paean to America's soulless wonderland and to gambling. Today the book is nothing more than a rare curiosity filled with huge print and photographs of casinos and scantily clad, large-breasted women, appropriate since portions of the book first appeared in *Playboy* magazine.

Did Mario Puzo really follow up his *Godfather* saga with this?

ANNE RICE

One of the best-selling authors in the world today, there are few who would argue that at the top of her form, Anne Rice is also one of the most lyrical and compelling. Unfortunately, none of that kept her from suffering a sophomore slump.

She had written from the age of five. Several novels were crafted and put aside. In 1972, her tiny daughter, Michele, died of leukemia, and one can read painful echoes of that experience in her descriptions of the angelic Claudia in *Interview With the Vampire*. The hardcover rights were bought for $12,000, and upon publication, in 1976, no less than seventy-five reviews poured in, most positive. The paperback rights went on the auction block and were purchased for $700,000. Paramount Pictures paid $150,000 for an option on the film rights.

Anne Rice was an instant publishing phenomenon—long before she would raise hell because Tom Cruise had been cast to play her most popular creation. And yet the film is sure to be a huge success. Nevertheless, though over time all of her books would sell extraordinarily well, at the beginning, there were no guarantees. Rather than follow up with another vampire novel, or even with another horror novel, Rice wrote a sensual tale of nineteenth-century New Orleans called *The Feast of All Saints*. Her advance was $150,000, and, almost as a self-fulfilling prophecy, the book did not approach the attention garnered and waves made by *Interview*.

Her third novel, *Cry to Heaven*, about *castrati* (singers who have been castrated to preserve a boyhood voice) drew half the advance of the previous book.

Her three erotic bondage novels were written under a pseudonym, as were *Belinda* and *Exit to Eden* (for which she received $35,000). In 1985, almost a full decade after *Interview*, *The Vampire Lestat* was published and became a hardcover best-seller. Rice received $100,000, only two-thirds of what she was paid for *The Feast of All Saints*.

By the time her next book, the third of *The Vampire Chronicles*, was published, her asking price had quintupled to $500,000. The following year, *The Mummy* was published, but the big news came with a two-book deal for *The Witching Hour*, and *Lasher* which combined brought her $5 million. The film rights to the former were brought for a million.

So those are the books, and the numbers. All of Anne Rice's works are dark, some of course far darker than others, so what is to explain the obvious success of her more horrific books versus the others? It is difficult to say. Not so difficult is the observation that whatever it was about *Interview With the Vampire*, whether it be the pain, the sensuality, or the plot that captivated readers, those elements continued to draw the audience into the rest of the story, and to the saga of the Mayfair witches with which it is slightly intermingled.

Upon the discovery that Anne Rice was their real author, the books she wrote as Anne Rampling and A. N. Roquelaure took a giant leap in sales. Of course, the more popular she becomes, the better her backlist sells. As such, though most authors would sell their souls, mothers, left legs, comic book collections to have a book sell as well as *The Feast of All Saints* has over a period of fifteen years, it was initially a sizable disappointment coming off the overwhelming success of *Interview With the Vampire*.

Today, Anne Rice continues to write, be read, and be paid in quantity.

More Fun Facts and Interesting Trivia

Ask for any of the books listed below at your bookstore. Or to order direct from the publisher, call 1-800-447-BOOK (MasterCard or Visa), or send a check or money order for the books purchased (plus $4.00 shipping and handling for the first book ordered and 75¢ for each additional book) to Carol Publishing Group, 120 Enterprise Avenue, Dept. 1584, Secaucus, NJ 07094.

Aardvarks to Zebras: A Menagerie of Facts, Fiction and Fantasy About the Wonderful World of Animals by Melissa S. Tulin
Illustrated with photographs & drawings
$14.95 paper   0-8065-1548-1   (CAN $20.95)

The Almanac of Fascinating Beginnings: From the Academy Awards to the Xerox Machine by Norman King
$9.95 paper   0-8065-1549-X   (CAN $13.95)

The Book of Totally Useless Information by Donald A. Voorhees
$7.95 paper   0-8065-1405-1   (CAN $9.95)

The Business Disasters Book of Days: The World's Greatest Financial Mishaps, Follies and Remarkable Events by Jill Herbers
$ 9.95 paper   0-8065-1585-6   (CAN $13.95)

The "Cheers" Trivia Book by Mark Wenger   Photographs throughout
$ 9.95 paper   0-8065-1482-5   (CAN $11.95)

The Complete Book of Sexual Trivia by Leslee Welch
$7.95 paper   0-8065-1347-0   (CAN $9.95)

The Encyclopedia of Popular Misconceptions: The Ultimate Debunker's Guide to Widely Accepted Fallacies by Ferris Johnsen
$9.95 paper   0-8065-1556-2   (CAN $13.95)

50 Greatest Conspiracies of All Time: History's Biggest Mysteries, Cover-ups and Cabals by Jonathan Vankin and John Whalen
$12.95 paper   0-8065-1576-7   (CAN $17.95)

Film Flubs: Memorable Movie Mistakes by Bill Givens
Illustrated with photographs throughout
$7.95 paper   0-8065-1161-3   (CAN $10.95)

Also available:
Son of Film Flubs by Bill Givens   Illustrated with photographs throughout
$7.95 paper   0-8065-1279-2   (CAN $10.95)

Film Flubs: The Sequel by Bill Givens   Illustrated with photographs throughout
$7.95 paper   0-8065-1360-8   (CAN $9.95)

George Washington Had No Middle Name: Strange Historical Facts by Patricia Lee Holt $5.95 paper   0-8065-1074-9   (CAN $7.95)

How a Fly Walks Upside Down and Other Curious Facts by Martin A. Goldwyn   Illustrations throughout
$7.95 paper   0-8065-1054-4   (CAN $10.95)

Light Your House With Potatoes: And 99 Other Off-the-wall Solutions to Life's Little Problems by Jay Kaye   Illustrations throughout
$7.95 paper   0-8065-1376-4   (CAN $9.95)

Old Wives' Tales: The Truth Behind Common Notions by Sue Castle
Illustrations throughout $7.95 paper   0-8065-1378-0   (CAN $9.95)

1001 Toughest TV Trivia Questions of All Time by Vincent Terrace
$9.95 paper   0-8065-1499-X   (CAN $11.95)

Peculiar Patents: A Collection of Unusual and Interesting Inventions from the Files of the U.S. Patent Office by Dr. Rick Feinberg
Illustrated throughout $9.95 paper   0-8065-1561-9   (CAN $13.95)

The "Seinfeld" Aptitude Test: Hundreds of Spectacular Questions on Minute Details from TV's Greatest Show About Absolutely Nothing by Beth B. Golub $8.95 paper   0-8065-1583-X   (CAN $12.95)

Why Do They Call It Topeka?: How Places Got Their Names by John W. Pursell $9.95 paper   0-8065-1588-0   (CAN $13.95)